YOUTH LEAGUE SOCCER SKILLS
MASTERING THE BALL

BY
MANNY SCHELLSCHEIDT

With
DEBORAH WICKENDEN

The Athletic Institute
North Palm Beach, FL 33480

A Word From The Publisher

This Sports Publication is but one item in a comprehensive list of sports instructional aids, such as video cassettes and 16 mm films, which are made available by The Athletic Institute. This book is part of a master plan which seeks to make the benefits of athletics, physical educational and recreation available to everyone. To obtain a free catalog, please write to the Athletic Institute at the address listed on the copyright page.

The Athletic Institute is a not-for-profit organization devoted to the advancement of athletics, physical education and recreation. The Institute believes that participation in athletics and recreation has benefits of inestimable value to the individual and to the community.

The nature and scope of the many Institute programs are determined by a Professional Advisory Committee, whose members are noted for their outstanding knowledge, experience and ability in the fields of athletics, physical education and recreation.

The Institute believes that through this book the reader will become a better performer, skilled in the fundamentals of this fine event. Knowledge and the practice necessary to mold knowledge into playing ability are the keys to real enjoyment in playing any game or sport.

John D. Riddle
President and Chief Executive Officer
The Athletic Institute

James Hotchkiss
Executive Director
The Athletic Institute

Table of Contents

Acknowledgments

I'd like to say thanks to those who have touched my life with their knowledge, patience, and love for the game: the coaches for whom I played in West Germany—Heinrich Becker, Heiner Schaffer, Albert Engelbracht, Hennes Weisweiler, and Detmar Cramer; my colleagues here in the United States—Jake Bradley, Angus McAlpine, and Bob Bradley; and last, but not least, the great number of players I have played with and coached. All I can say is, you are all wonderful.

I'd also like to thank my collaborator, Deborah Wickenden. It is not easy for two people to put their heads together and write a book on soccer. I am most happy and pleased to have worked with Debbie, because not only is she a wonderful writer, but as a former soccer player herself she has a good understanding of the game, which may have made it much easier for her to understand and write about my philosophy.

Manfred Schellscheidt

Introduction

Youth Sports: Benefits and Responsibilities for the Athlete and Coach

Benefits of Participating in Sports

Sports for children have become so popular that an estimated 20 million American children between the ages of six and sixteen play one or more sports each year. This tremendous interest suggests that parents and children believe that competitive athletics contribute positively to children's development. Such a wholesale endorsement may be misleading, however, unless it is counterbalanced by the sobering statistic that approximately 70 percent of the children drop out of organized sports programs by age fifteen. Many of the children who drop out are the ones who could benefit most from organized sports if directed by competent coaches. Thus, every coach, parent and athlete should answer the questions, "What are the benefits of competitive sports for children?" and "How can I be sure that these benefits are available to all children who participate in youth sports?"

Clearly, sports can have both positive and negative effects on children, but positive results can occur only if coaches and athletes conduct themselves in responsible ways. Although many of the benefits are immediately detectable and of a short-term nature, the most sought-after and important contributions of sports to total development are those that last far beyond the athlete's playing days.

In order for the benefits of sports to be available for all children, they must be identified, valued and included in their practices and games. Following are some of the benefits that are most commonly associated with children's sports participation:

- developing various sports skills
- learning how to cooperate and compete

- developing a sense of achievement, which leads to a positive self image
  - developing an interest in and a desire to continue participation in sports during adulthood
  - developing independence
  - developing social skills
  - learning to understand and express emotion, imagination, and appreciation for what the body can do
  - developing speed, strength, endurance, coordination, flexibility, and agility
  - developing leadership skills
  - learning to make decisions and accept responsibilities

The Role of the Coach in Youth Sports

The coach of young athletes is the single most important adult in all of children's athletics. Other adults, such as officials and administrators, have important responsibilities, too, but no task is as important as that of the coach, who must guide young children physically, socially and emotionally as they grow from childhood through adolescence into adulthood.

The youth sports coach is required to play many roles. Most prominent among these are being a teacher and an instructor of skills, a friend who listens and offers advice, a substitute parent when the athlete's mother or father is not available or accessible, a medical advisor who knows when and when not to administer first aid and emergency care, a disciplinarian who rewards and corrects behavior, and a cheerleader who provides encouragement when everything goes wrong.

The age and development level of the athletes will determine how frequently the coach is asked to assume the various roles. Indeed, coaches may find themselves switching roles minute by minute as the fast-moving, complex nature of a contest calls for different responsibilities. The coach's responsibilities in each of the most common roles are discussed in the following sections.

The Coach As a Teacher

Although all of the coach's responsibilities are important, none is more important than being a good teacher. No matter how adept a coach is in other roles, these successes cannot overcome the harm caused by bad teaching. What then, are the characteristics of a good teacher?

Good teachers know what they are attempting to teach and are able to **select appropriate content** for the various levels of ability of their team members. Good teachers are **well organized,** both for the long-term season and in their daily practice and game plans. Good teacher are also **interested in the progress** of all their team members, including those who are inept and slow-learning. In summary, good teachers must love their athletes and their sport so much that practice sessions and games are joyful experiences for coaches and athletes.

The Coach As a Friend

Children play sports for many reasons, but one of the most frequently cited is that they like to be with friends and make new friends. Often, the most important role of the coach is just being a friend to a child who has none.

Being a friend to a friendless child often requires initiative and extra work for a coach, because such children are often unskilled and may have personality characteristics which make it difficult for other children to like them. Often the attention and affection by a coach is a sufficient stimulus for other team members to become more accepting, too. Regardless of the effort required, the coach must ensure that every child feels accepted as a member of the team.

The coach as a friend must be enthusiastic about sports and the participation of all children. Good friends are motivators who reward players with compliments and positive instruction instead of concentrating on errors. Good friends make children feel good about playing sports.

The Coach As a Substitute Parent

Nearly 50 percent of today's young athletes are likely to live in single-parent families. Whether or not coaches want the role of being a substitute parent, they are likely to acquire it. Even those children who live with both parents are apt to need the advice of their coach occasionally.

One of the most useful functions of the coach as a substitute parent is simply to listen to the child's problems. Frequently, the mere presence of an adult listener who inserts an occasional question to assist the child in clarifying the problem is all that is needed. As a coach, you must be careful not to judge the appropriateness of a parent's actions. In most instances the problems between parents and children are simply misunderstandings about children's desires and responsibilities. Such misunderstandings can usually be resolved by discussion, persuasion and compromise. However, in situations where parental actions are resulting in physical or mental abuse, the coach should contact professional counselors who are equipped to deal with such problems.

The Coach As Medical Advisor

Medical problems should be left to medical personnel who are equipped to deal with them. However, as a coach you are usually the first person at the scene of a youth sports injury and, therefore, are obligated to provide or obtain the necessary first aid. In addition, your judgment is likely to be called upon in situations where an injury has occurred and a decision must be made about whether the athlete should return to practice or competition.

A prudent policy for you is to resist making decisions which others are more qualified to make. You should seek the advice of medical personnel when injuries occur. Encourage your athletes to report aches, pains and injuries that are likely to impede their performance. Despite the emphasis on short-term objectives, your job is to safeguard the health of the athletes so that they are able to participate fully in physical activity well beyond the childhood years.

The Coach As Disciplinarian

One of the most frequently cited values of youth sports is their alleged contribution to the behavior and moral development of athletes. However, there are instances in children's sports where coaches and athletes have behaved in socially unacceptable ways. Obviously, attitudes and behaviors can be affected both positively and negatively in sports.

The first step to being a good disciplinarian is to establish the rules that will govern the athletes' behavior. These rules are more likely to be accepted and followed if the athletes have a voice in identifying them. Secondly, you must administer the rules fairly to all athletes. Desirable behavior must be enforced and undesirable actions must be corrected.

The Coach As a Cheerleader

Young athletes are likely to make numerous mental and physical errors as they attempt to learn specific skills. For that reason, their coaches must be tolerant of mistakes and eager to applaud any actions that represent improvement in performance.

Young athletes respond well to praise that is earned and given sincerely. Conversely, they are not very tolerant of criticism, especially when it occurs in association with a coach's expectations that are beyond their capacities or abilities. You must know your athletes so well that your requests are likely to result in a high ratio of successes to failures. When you choose tasks that are challenging but are likely to be done successfully you are in a position to be a **positive coach.** Positive coaches are likely to have fewer discipline problems than coaches who expect too much and then focus on inappropriate behavior. Being a positive coach is a good way to build the self-esteem that all young athletes need in order to feel successful about their sports participation.

The Role of the Athlete

A successful youth sports experience places demands on athletes as well as coaches. These responsibilites should be stated so that athletes and their parents understand what is expected of them. Some of the most important responsibilities of athletes are as follows:

- treat all teammates and opponents with respect and dignity
- obey all team and league rules
- give undivided attention to instruction of techniques, skills and drills
- always practice and play with a clear mind
- report all injuries to the coach for further medical evaluation
- discourage rule violations by teammates or opponents
- play under emotional control at all times
- avoid aggressive acts of self-destruction
- compliment good performances of teammates and opponents
- return to play when an injury is completely rehabilitated

Summary

Youth sports are designed to provide benefits to both athletes and coaches. However, these benefits cannot be obtained in the absence of clearly defined responsibilities. When both coaches and athletes accept and carry out the responsibilities defined in this introduction, then the benefits of youth sports participation are likely to be realized.

Vern Seefeldt, Ph.D.
Director
Youth Sports Institute
Michigan State University

I. About Soccer

When my colleague, Angus McAlpine, and I took a United States team of eighteen- and nineteen-year-old boys to play in a qualifying tournament in Guatemala, we had an experience I will never forget. All the teams were fighting for one spot in the Under-Twenty Youth World Cup competition, and nationalistic fever was running pretty high. Our third game was against the host country, Guatemala, and the stadium was packed with a capacity crowd of 64,000 booing and whistling hostile fans. Fences and men armed with machine guns kept tight security, and an underground tunnel ran from the locker room to a spot behind one of the goals to allow us safe passage onto the field. Understandably, the boys were quite nervous, but they settled in and played a great game, beating Guatemala by a score of 3-1. And that's when it happened. The crowd rose to its feet and gave us a standing ovation. Hatred had turned into respect and admiration. We had beaten them at their own game, and we were now accepted as a member of the largest family in the world—the soccer family.

The Nature of the Game

Soccer is a process of solving little problems, and the most successful players are the ones who work with their teammates to do this. The problems can be general. How does a team get out of the backfield? How do the players get through the midfield? How do they get a shot off? If the other team gets the ball, how can the players be kept away from the goal? Will the attacking players help defend as they are coming back? Will the defending players help attack when they steal the ball? What is it like to defend in front of the goal versus the midfield and the offensive end?

The problems can be more specific, more individual. Is a heel pass going to be most effective in this situation? Should the defensive player charge an approaching opponent? Is it better to mark a man tightly or to shift away slightly in order to help another teammate?

These are some of the very different elements of soccer that a player can only figure out when he plays. A coach can talk all he wants to about tactics, but the ultimate teacher is the game itself. Playing is all that is needed to give a youngster sensitivity to the nuances and subtleties of this beautiful sport.

Because this is the case, this book is not concerned with teaching the strategy of playing soccer. Instead, it presents exercises that will give both beginning and advanced players a vehicle through which to learn the important elements of the game. Many of these exercises place the players in a gamelike situation, so that their tactical skills will develop alongside their physical skills.

A Matter of Semantics

I like to use the word *exercise* rather than *drill,* which to me has a bad taste to it. It sounds military and doesn't incorporate the idea that an exercise can be adapted in many different ways. Using the word drill implies that there is one way to do it and that is the only way. That is not to say that we don't need the repetition. There is no question that repeated contact with a ball will help a player's skills. The most basic tasks must be practiced over and over again to the point where they can be done effortlessly at top speed and under the pressure of a game situation. What we don't need is the inflexibility that comes with the word drill.

Learning the Game

The game of soccer appeals to a certain kind of person, and a player with a true love of the game will have an experience that goes far beyond merely kicking a ball up and down the field. My case is unusual, I know, but soccer opened doors for me that never would have been there otherwise. I was in the United States briefly and hooked up with a soccer team just so that I could get in some training. I didn't want to be out of shape when I returned home. I started practicing with this team on a Wednesday. By that Sunday, I had a team jersey, was playing in a game, and had been asked to stay on for a year. Twenty-six years later, I'm still living here.

As I said, experiences like this won't happen to everyone. The point I'm trying to make, however, is that not everyone can play soccer. It appeals to a certain type of person—although that type can take many forms. There are some who play with sheer talent and are very gifted, and there are others who get to it by more of a learning process. No matter what the process, it is usually the more dedicated youngster who will become the better player. The most crucial quality in a developing soccer player is the ability and willingness to learn.

The player who has the ability to understand the game and combine this knowledge with his physical capabilities is the real soccer player. It doesn't matter if another player can juggle the ball twice as many times; if he can't get something done out on the field, he won't be much use to a team. This is not so obvious in the youngest players, because none of them have learned soccer tactics at this point. At this stage, it is the strongest and most coordinated player who makes the difference to a team. Later, however, the player's tactical abilities will show up clearly. This is already an example of playing to a player's strengths.

One of the tactical abilities that I'm referring to is a player's comprehension of the relative strengths and weaknesses of the people he plays with and of the team as a whole. For instance, if nobody on the team can hit a forty-yard ball or a fifty-yard ball, then the smart player will not run halfway down the field to an open area; he knows the ball won't come to him.

As an aside, this example shows why the little fellows—the five-, six-, and seven-year-olds—are all in one lump. The longest kick on that team can reach maybe twenty yards. The youngsters are forced to hover around the ball if they want to touch it at all. Already, at this young age, their soccer instincts are developing. I'm not saying it's a good thing for them to clump, but it is natural. The way to break that up is to play smaller games—three against three or two against two.

Good playing is based on what the game or the exercise demands. A player must know that he has to run when it counts, and he must have a constant reading of the flow of the game in order to be in the best possible position at all times. He must always keep in mind that attack and defense can come in many forms. For example, defense can be accomplished by tight marking, high pressure, and the ability to tackle, or it can be done through smart playing and the laying of traps for the opponent, where the player is lulled into a false sense of security and the ball can be stolen from him easily. Similarly, the attack can take different forms, depending on the player.

Every player on the field should consider himself both an attacker and a defender. The defender who easily succeeds in shutting down an opponent's forward should not be satisfied with leaving matters at that. He must now become a player who supports the attack to the fullest extent of his capacity. A good attack starts at the very moment a team gains the ball and, for the most part, that happens in a team's defensive third of the field. At this moment, the team has the greatest attacking advantage because a good number of opposing players are likely to be in bad defensive positions. It now is imperative to take advantage of the situation and move forward swiftly, without allowing the opposing team time to regain safe defensive positions.

With this in mind, it is obvious that the first pass forward will most likely put more opposing players out of position than the second or third. Therefore—the point I am trying to make—the defending players had better know about starting a counterattack. As a result of this, we can say that good attacking begins with our defenders, or anyone who wins the ball, and, similarly, that good defending begins with our forwards, or anyone who loses the ball.

Unwritten Rules

There are a few "rules" of soccer that won't be found in an official manual, but it is imperative that every soccer player learn them. Take, for instance, uncontrolled rebounds. These are absolutely forbidden. Even if a player cannot settle a ball cleanly, he must jump on every ball that gets away. Chasing uncontrolled, loose balls, however, will slow the game down, and the habit means that the player has become a slave of the ball, which makes for the sloppy, uncontrolled playing we see so often in high school soccer.

Another vitally important rule is to meet the ball. A player who waits for the ball to come to him will lose it 99 percent of the time, because if he doesn't meet it, a defender will. It is difficult to impart the need for meeting the ball to younger players, because it's much harder for them to receive a ball when they are running onto it than when they wait for it. The lesson has to come from the game. If a player is beaten to the ball five times in a row, he will eventually realize that if he doesn't run there as well he'll never get it. And if he doesn't realize this, then he is probably not capable of becoming a top-notch soccer player: he can't learn from the game.

This is a great example of how players become smart. Meeting the ball is not instinctive or natural—it goes against a degree of laziness and a lack of confidence that typify most beginning players—but it can seem natural when a player develops good soccer sense. Good habits like this will set the good soccer players apart.

Finally, another rule is that a player must come to the rescue of a teammate. Every player must constantly be on his way to support the ball. This is a vitally important unwritten rule. When a teammate gets the ball, a player can't just sit back and casually observe the play. (We call this becoming a ball watcher.) He must immediately put himself in a position to help. That doesn't necessarily mean that if a forward has the ball, the defenseman must come sprinting all the way up the field, but he should move up somewhat, in as good a supporting manner as his position allows. It also means that the other forwards are obligated to make themselves available, too. Now the teammate has options.

In defense, supporting the ball is just as important. If a player on the right side goes out to meet the ball, the player on the left side must shift toward the middle to help fill in the open spaces. Now the forwards must come back to receive a pass. Everyone should be alert and moving, in relation to where the ball is on the field.

Games That Children Play

There really is no age limit to when a child should begin playing soccer, and by that I mean getting a feel for the ball, kicking it, and touching it. In this country, we put youngsters into organized soccer as soon as they show an interest in playing, but that is not necessarily the best thing to do. In most other countries, they play soccer at the same young age, but they aren't involved in it in an organized sense until much later. If children are left alone, they learn the skills of soccer all by themselves.

It begins when there is a ball in the house; perhaps a parent or a sibling has played. The youngster begins by simply running with the ball; he is already learning dribbling skills. Then the child runs with the ball and takes a shot. When two players show up, the first thing they do is set up two goals, not too far from each other, and they instinctively practice the two most essential parts of the game—shooting and defending. Center forward and goalie positions are already covered with only two players. Nobody needs to tell them that. The game is all about scoring and about keeping the ball from going into the net. That final drama is the starting point for a beginning soccer player.

Then how do we build from there? Dribbling and shooting have started to develop, and now it becomes dribbling and shooting in such a way that the other person cannot get the ball. Deception and faking are already happening. The idea is to mislead the other person so that he can be beaten.

As soon as there are more than two players, passing and receiving come into play. Now the youngsters can move the ball around in another way. Tactics change. The game of soccer will naturally evolve.

Street soccer is a phenomenon in other countries that we really need to bring to America, because it enhances the soccer personality more than anything else. And the reason, believe it or not, is because there is no coach. All the coaching is within the group, among the players themselves. The only teacher is the game.

True, the children in other countries do have another "teacher," in the sense that they have role models that we don't have. They can watch the game being played at a good level by the first-division players and get a sense of what their own play should look like. Nonetheless, I still maintain that one of the reasons why soccer is so far behind in this country is that the children don't have enough opportunity just to learn from the game.

Ages will often be quite lopsided in these street games, where a five-year-old plays with a ten-year-old. Of course, half the time, the five-year-old is just chasing the action around, never getting a kick at the ball. But even this will help him become smart. He is not big enough to assert himself physically, so the only way he can get to play is to develop a good sense for the game. When parents place their children in organized soccer from day one, they often deprive them of this educational process.

Also, coaches all too often force young children to do more than they are able to do, making them do exercises and play games that only older children are capable of performing. Young children playing eleven against eleven on a full-sized field is a travesty. They are not capable of that, and so it becomes a waste of time. As I mentioned earlier, when the children are young, both the group and the playing area should be small. A small group means more contact with the ball, and that has to be one of the top priorities at this age. This is the time when skills develop. If a player is not a master of the ball by age fourteen then chances are he never will be. Developing better skills after that age becomes more difficult because a person's learning process has slowed, and at the same time the competition is much fiercer.

The coaching aspects in soccer are somewhat limited as compared to other sports, because the youngster really has to find out the rights and the wrongs on his own when he plays. Some players have developed sensitivity to the rights and wrongs and what works and what doesn't work; others will never develop this sensitivity, no matter how long they play. They will never really make any progress.

Good skills can be defined as the ability to control and move the ball in every possible way. The whole body is meant to be in the picture. A player should be able to receive the ball wherever it hits him—on the head, on the chest, on the thigh, on the stomach, on the outside of the foot, on the inside of the foot. Any part of the body should be ready to receive the ball. There are different ways of releasing the ball, moving it on to the next person in such a manner that it results in a quality pass—a ball with the right weight on it. Any part of the body, again, can move the ball to the next person, but the choice is quite delicate. In the end, the selection makes the difference between the skillful player and the one who just doesn't quite have that kind of feel and touch.

Analyzing a Player's Ability

Physical, technical, and tactical abilities are developed in conjunction with one another. Each relies on the others and complements the others. A physically smaller player often compensates for his size through marvelous skills, great vision, and a good tactical sense. For him, the physical handicap present from day one has forced development in the other two areas. On the flip side, a player who is strong and fast will all too often rely on these gifts and not develop either touch or smarts. A good, competitive environment will create demands in all three areas—physical, technical, and tactical—and will count most in a soccer player's development. The essential components within each of these areas are as follows:

1. Physical Ability (Fitness)
   Strength
   Endurance
   Speed
   Mobility
   Agility
   Flexibility
2. Technical Ability (Technique)
   Control
   Touch
   Coordination
3. Tactical Ability (Soccer Brain)
   Decision Making
   Sensitivity
   Playing it Smart

Physical Ability

The player must be in shape. No matter how many skills a player has, they won't do him any good if he can't beat an opponent to the ball or if he has to collapse, exhausted, on the sideline after five minutes of running. In order to use his skills, the player needs strong legs and the endurance to run up and down the field—he needs conditioning. Speed may also be included as part of this area, but speed in soccer is a very debatable item. A player who can run down the field with blinding speed will win the admiration of the spectators, but is he really a quick soccer player? He could be falling over the ball because he is running *too* fast. He may not be good at receiving the ball and have to retrap every ball that comes to him several times instead of being able to settle the ball at his feet immediately and get on with the play. He loses an extra second every time he has to retrap a ball, which turns him into a very slow player, despite his sprinting ability. So speed alone does not make one a fast soccer player.

Technical Ability

The second of the three elements of a good soccer player is sheer technical ability. But technical skill can come in many forms. Some players, for instance, have a dazzling mastery of the ball and can really entertain the spectators. Other players may have an accurate pass that never misses or an ability to trap the ball cleanly every time. Then there is the defender who has a tremendous knack and timing for beating people to the ball. It is just as important to beat someone else to the ball as it is for somebody to flip the ball over his head. So there are many ways of defining technical skill. Once a player has the requisite footwork and bodywork that he needs in order to control the game, he is no longer a slave to the ball.

Tactical Ability

The third way to come out on top comes from being smart about things. A player can be extremely effective merely by getting the most out of a little and finding a way to get a job done. If a player doesn't know what he's going to do, he has to take time to figure it out. That makes him a very slow player. If he were a smart player, he would have it all figured out ahead of time and could deliver the ball to a teammate in one stroke. This is not to deny the point that tactically at times a player might need to hold onto the ball. One skill lies in knowing *when* to hold it and in knowing *how* to hold it, defending the ball one on one if nobody is open. A smart player will know how to create opportunities and will have the presence to calmly take advantage of them. This is the gift that we call a big-game mentality.

To seek improvement in one area without involving the other two may not bring the best results. We may emphasize technique during

an exercise in order to polish ball control, but for there to be a real measure of improvement, we need to put it back into a gamelike situation. In addition, fitness obtained in an isolated way will not necessarily guarantee that a player will be fit for soccer.

The degree of excellence in the three areas will be largely responsible for the capacity of a player and his level of performance. Some players are stronger in one area than another, which is to be expected. Fortunately, as long as there is a basic level of competence in all three areas, strength in one can overcome a weakness in another. If a player has the tactical and technical ability, for instance, but lacks endurance, he can make good use of the ball and let the ball do most of the work for him. The measurement of a good player comes from adding the three components together. That will be the level of play that he can account for in a match as one player for his team.

These three areas spill over into the personality of a team as well. Some teams try to win by virtue of superior physical conditioning. (They give the impression of having two or three more players on the field than their opponents.) Their aim is to wear the other team down by being everywhere at once. Others display quite brilliant skills that delight the onlookers, almost as if they're performing magic with the ball. (Qualities like this often develop in regions of hot climates and the hard or poor ground conditions that go along with them.) Two or three players are capable of carrying the action while their team-mates can pace themselves. And some teams win because they are much cleverer at outwitting their opponents. They can anticipate better, and they have a keener instinct about when to pass, shoot, or dribble.

One-on-One Duels

Each player will always have someone out on the field whom, for the most part, he is playing against. This statement should not be interpreted rigidly, but, in general, each player will have an opponent whom he deals with more often than any other. The goal for each player stepping out on the field should be to win the individual duel with this opponent. Whether he has the ability to succeed at this is another issue; but winning this duel must be his objective. If the player does win, he becomes a plus player for the team, meaning, in essence, that he's an attacker. He is already establishing an advantage in his section of the field. If the majority of the players on the team succeed individually, then most likely they will become the winning team.

If something works for a player, then he should be allowed to do it. Getting the job done—winning a duel—is the bottom line, and it doesn't really matter how a player goes about it (provided, of course, that it's within the rules). He should be allowed to have his own style. For instance, a good defender can come in many different forms. Some are just hard-nosed players that get in there and tackle. Others are so smart that they succeed chiefly by laying traps. They fool the other team so badly that to someone watching it looks as if the opponents just gave up the ball. That's the beauty of soccer. No two players are alike and no game can ever be a copy of the one that was just played.

The Soccer Brain

Fitness in soccer means both fitness of the body and fitness of the mind. A player with a soccer brain plays it smart by using his technical and physical qualities to their best advantage. Awareness, alertness, and anticipation have to be present at all times. Sensing the intentions and bluffs of opponents, as well as recognizing the specific strengths and weaknesses in an opposing player, are qualities all good players must have, but mental toughness and a good level of discipline are just as important. One of the hardest things for a player to do is to mentally stay in the game at all times. Quite often, players lose their concentration at some point over the ninety minutes. They are always looking for breaks or they drift out of the action. This factor alone accounts for most of the breakdowns and mistakes.

When I started out as coach at Seton Hall, I had no idea what to expect from the players. The first practice, I decided, would not include long runs or hard sprints because I could work on their

*The Quintessential
Soccer Brain*

physical development later; for the first practice, I wanted to see the level of their skill development. I had them play very demanding, one-touch small-sided games for almost the entire training session. By the end, a couple of players came up to me and asked if they could just do some running. I couldn't believe it! I'd never heard of players who *wanted* to run. But what I had done was to force them to use their brains nonstop. They had had to be alert at every stage of the training session, and now, mentally, they were quite exhausted. So I sent them off on their run, and they came back feeling great.

When a player cannot keep his mind on the game, he has what I call a mental breakdown. He is not connecting to the flow of the ball that constantly tells him that he must adjust his position. Mental fitness is something entirely different from physical fitness, because sometimes a player can walk and still be mentally in the game. Of course, sometimes he also must jog to keep up and sometimes he has to sprint as fast as he can. The level of play depends on the flow of the game and the pressure from the other team. No matter what, at all times, a player must be thinking, moving, and adjusting.

This concentration is one of the hardest things to teach. When a five-year-old wakes up in the morning, he doesn't automatically have it. It has to be learned, and a player will never be great if he can't stay tuned in. Great players always know where to be, and they always know how to get into the right spot before the other player gets there. That is why some relatively slow players can actually be very fast players. Their anticipation, their reading of the game, and their skill all compensate for their lack of speed.

It's wonderful to watch little kids and already see, in the rough, qualities like that. From there, it becomes just a matter of pushing them forward. In this sense, being a professional is not a matter of age; it is a degree of excellence. A twelve-year-old could be a "professional" in his own right. He has achieved the top level of excellence, mentally and physically, for his age. He can play soccer, period. Obviously he is small and can only play, physically, at a reduced level, but I have seen a number of games where twelve-year-olds put on a display that was soccer at its best. What I'm trying to get across is that there is no age limit to coming to terms with what's going on out there. There are some older players who are still just as inadequate as they were when they were ten years old.

Because this mental toughness is so consuming, it is important that a player not have to burden his mind with physical matters as well. All the physical actions, whatever the skills that are demanded of a player, have to be subconscious, instinctive reactions. This, finally, is where the training session enters the picture.

The Training Session

A training session is a time to solve problems, but a coach certainly should not try to include every single problem, skill, and drill in his training session. Often a coach strives for variety in order to keep the youngsters interested, but by doing so, he deprives the players of intensive work on a problem. Instead of galloping through all the skills, he can merely vary the exercises and still keep the focus of the practice the same. There has to be a balance between keeping the training session interesting and getting the point across. The coach should focus on one or two or three of the skills—really let the youngsters get a feel for them—and then leave some time for playing.

How would a session break down? First, there should be the warm-up. This should include light running or aerobic exercise, stretching, and ball exercises. Every player should have a ball, and the exercises should allow each one to touch the ball in every possible way.

I always like to stress the importance of using the ball; this even includes having youngsters use their hands. By handling the ball in every possible way, they develop coordination. Before they can become athletes, they need to feel a rhythm. They ought to have a

feel for the bounce. I also have no problem with children playing many different sports, because they are mostly ball games and they all require that kind of eye/foot or eye/hand coordination. With this experience, a child can more easily become a master of the ball.

Granted, it is possible to have effective exercises without the ball—and I have included some in this book—but their use should be limited. If a coach can detect a specific area of physical weakness in a player, then maybe he could send the player to the weight room or have him run extra laps. But unless there is a major weakness, a coach can always find strengthening exercises that include a ball and a player's own body weight or his partner's. A player doesn't need dumbbells or irons to build up his muscles. It is much more fun and much more appealing for people who love soccer to work out with the ball. I have yet to find soccer players who have a love for pumping iron.

The first part of the warm-up should be active, something to get the muscles warm. A cold muscle should never be stretched. As the players loosen up through moving, they can begin stretching. In other words, the warm-up should be a combination of jogging and stretching and jogging and stretching, always with the ball if possible. This way, the youngsters are warming up both their bodies and their soccer brains.

The coach can have maybe two or three specified stretching times, when certain muscle groups are identified and stretched. The older players, who are more aware of what their bodies need, can take another two or three minutes on their own if they need it while the other players move and warm up in different ways. Usually at this age there is no need for direction in a warm-up, but the younger players have to be told what to stretch and when to do it, and when to move the ball around and how to go about moving it around. Approximately ten to fifteen minutes should be set aside for this.

Ball work on specific skills develops nicely from the warm-up. A coach can even tailor the warm-up to match the type of skills that he plans to be working on for the rest of the practice. Ball work should last twenty to thirty minutes.

Finally, there should be approximately half an hour for small-sided games and then half an hour for the scrimmage. This book is designed to follow a training session. The chapters begin with the warm-up, go through the ball handling, and finally end with the games.

II. Coaching Philosophy

The Parent As Coach

If players are motivated to learn soccer—this is generally the case at the high school and college levels—then one coach is sufficient for a large group. Unfortunately, this is not true for the beginners, the young children. They need much more attention; otherwise it will merely become social hour on the field. With the youngest group, it is often good to have one coach for every four or five kids so that they can get individual instruction. Obviously, in most communities this can't be done—there are far too few volunteers as it is. But losing the players' attention is one of the biggest mistakes a coach can make, both for his own sanity and for the children's budding interest in soccer.

This is one of the reasons a well-organized, fast-paced training session is so important. If a coach has a variety of activities planned, especially enjoyable ones that involve playing a game, then he can get the youngsters so caught up in playing that they forget that they are learning. This book, in addition to providing exercises for coaches at all levels, is meant to help the parent—who is forced out of the stands against his or her will—plan training sessions that are both helpful and fun.

These parents, the ones who only become coaches because of the lack of manpower, immediately think, "But I don't know anything about the game." My reply to that is, "Well, you're just the right person." As I have tried to stress, at the early levels—ages five, six, seven, and maybe even eight—we don't want the coaches to coach too much. We want them to be supervisors. As long as the coach can explain the basic laws and skills of soccer, then the game, in the end, will do all the teaching that is necessary.

In fact, sometimes parents can do more harm than good when they try to get too involved and don't know exactly what they're talking about. They are better off just letting the kids experience the game.

We do have a somewhat dangerous mentality in the United States—perhaps translated to us from other sports—of viewing the coach as the mastermind who makes all the decisions. In soccer, that is just not possible. The players have to develop their own minds. They have to develop their soccer brains, because once the game starts at the opening whistle, the players are on their own. Actually, except in youth soccer, coaching from the sidelines is not permitted. The players take over.

However, in youth soccer, no matter where you go, when the referee starts the game by blowing the whistle, most of these youth-league coaches start coaching. This just tells me that the coach has not managed to get his lessons taught in training. All these things should be squared away in the practice session, so that by the time the game comes around, the players know what they have to do.

Creating a Team

The key to coaching lies in recognizing the strengths and weaknesses of each player and then figuring out the best formation for the players so that their strengths are emphasized and their weaknesses minimized or compensated for by their teammates. The ability of the players to influence the flow of the game in such a way that it plays into their hands and maximizes their team's strengths, both individual and collective, is the art of winning. But a coach should always keep in mind that he must find the right balance between, on the one hand, shaping and organizing his players and, on the other hand, encouraging freedom of expression and individual style.

That is not to say that a coach shouldn't develop these players' strengths to their maximum potential and improve upon their weaknesses, but he should be careful how he goes about doing it. Skill that is obtained in an isolated manner often makes for a slower player. The player is used to no-pressure situations and often spends more time than he should on the ball. A good player will need fewer touches on the ball, and this, obviously, speeds up his game.

The Mental Picture

I have yet to go to a coaching clinic where one of the coaches hasn't asked the national coach, who is lecturing, to tell the group what he wants in a player. They want him to describe the qualities that they should be looking for when they go to the trenches. It sounds like a good question but it isn't, because if the coach doesn't already have a clear picture, he's in trouble. A mental concept like this cannot be passed on through talk. It's impossible to diagram; it's something that a coach either knows or doesn't know.

For a coach, it is vitally important to have a good mental picture of what world-class soccer is all about, even if he is starting his coaching with a five-year-old. If the coach doesn't have that final picture in mind, it will become very difficult for him to take soccer in its basic form and bring it up to the professional level.

Unfortunately, there is a flip side to this. Often a coach will have seen the Cosmos play, for example, and he will take this final version of soccer development and try to make his young players play that way. That is surely not the way to go about it. Learning soccer, like learning anything, is a developmental process that starts with the most basic elements and then works up to the more complicated ones.

It is also, as I've said before, very important to go with the natural ability, with the natural flow. I don't believe it is possible to dismantle a player and make him over again in the image of "the perfect soccer player," because all coaches and all players are different. What works for one could be disastrous for another.

In the tactical realm, it's the same. It doesn't help merely to tell a player how to do something. One of the things a coach can do, however, is to confront the player with the problem and tell him to solve it. If a coach lets the player use his own ingenuity, he will pick up tactics much better, and he will learn in a way that is best for his style of play. It is important for every coach to understand that no two players are alike and no single game can be a copy of another.

Therefore, for a coach to diagram (we have a tremendous urge, especially in the United States, to diagram) the game and the way to play it is ridiculous. It is impossible to predict how a game will work out. Everything depends on the ingenuity of the individuals who step onto the field and the way they deal with the game.

The Personal Experience

Playing the game of soccer is an ongoing personal experience that needs to be dealt with as it presents itself. Reading a book or listening to a coach describe something can be worthwhile, but it is nothing compared to the personal experience the young soccer player gets from actually playing the game.

When the game is over, the player has learned something that he will remember, something that will clue him in to what it was all about, what it was like. Unfortunately, if that picture does not match the coach's analysis, there will be a conflict. Players will hear something from the coach that is completely different from what they thought they had experienced. This is one more reason why it is not necessarily best for an inexperienced coach to talk too much.

That doesn't mean, however, that the coach, who has a chance to see the whole picture from the outside, should just keep quiet when he knows something can be fixed. But he should always temper his criticisms by pointing out areas in the game where the player did well. After that, the coach can mention that there are things that need to be worked on.

It is even tougher when a part of the game that normally displays the player's strengths was not played quite well enough to have an impact. In this case, it may be better for the player to work on that strength area than on the weaknesses, so that least in some sense the player can be a factor in the game. A coach has to recognize that developing strengths may sometimes be even more important than overcoming weaknesses. And he can provide positive reinforcement when he uses the natural talents of a player and expands them before starting work on something that the youngster may find hard to handle.

Matchlike Conditions

Not too long ago, a commission of ten people went to the World Cup to examine the development of soccer. They came away saying that the player of the future can still be improved on. I firmly believe this is true because all too much fitness and skill is obtained in isolated conditions away from the soccer field, and that doesn't really fit in in the end. Players need to practice under matchlike conditions.

Skill that is learned in an isolated manner often leads to spending too much time on the ball, and that makes for a slower player. If, however, the player learns a skill while playing in a situation that is more like a game, then he will perhaps learn to perform that skill at game-level speed.

However, there has to be progression. A coach cannot always jump directly into a tough matchlike situation. First of all, the youngsters would never learn the basics, and second, they would be exhausted before too much time had elapsed. There are four ways that a coach can bring an exercise from the most simple (least demanding) to the most matchlike: (1) by increasing movement, (2) by decreasing touches on the ball, (3) by limiting space, and (4) by adding a goal. And he should use at least one of these—and often several of them—for *every* exercise. A coach should always be thinking about how to move a skill from one level to the next, how to change an exercise so that it demands a higher level of play. It is not enough for the players to sit back and admire their handiwork. There is always room for improvement.

Granted, a coach is more limited when he is working with the youngest players, because they just don't have the skill to move along certain progressions. However, some of these progressions will work for any age, and it is up to the coach to decide what is best for his team and to implement these practices.

Moving Progression

In this sense the training of skills can be broken down into three levels: standing, moving, and match speed.

Standing:	No Pressure
Moving:	Limited Pressure
Match Speed:	Match Pressure

Using heading as an example, the standing stage would involve a server and a header. The server would toss the ball to the header, who would head it back. If the header moves backward across the field and the server tosses the ball while he is moving, then the players have progressed to the second stage. Finally, if the header is forced to leap into the air each time he heads the ball, he has moved up to match-level conditions.

In the beginning he simply works on the basic elements of heading. If the coach merely ends the exercise there, the player would never know how to use this finely honed skill in a game. Likewise, if the coach lets the player work only at match-level heading, then the player wouldn't get a solid grasp on the basics. It would be like trying to race in the Indy 500 before getting a driver's license.

Touches on the Ball

Another progression that increases the difficulty of the skill involves how many times a player is allowed to touch the ball: unlimited, two touches, or one touch. In this sense, one stage isn't necessarily more matchlike than the other, but in order to be effective on the field, a player must be able to do them all. He should also be able to switch from using his dominant foot to using his weaker foot.

Unlimited Touches:	No Pressure
Two Touches:	Limited Pressure
One Touch:	Match Pressure

At first a coach should make it relatively easy until his players get an idea of what's going on. Once they have mastered or almost mastered one skill, then a coach should bring in the demand that it be two touches and then one touch.

FIG. 2-1A *Server and header. Header standing.*

FIG. 2-1B *Header running backwards.*

FIG. 2-1C *Header running backwards and jumping.*

By decreasing the touches, the coach is increasing the speed. This sends out the right message. We hope that a player will realize that mastering a skill does not mean that more time can be spent on the ball. It really means that now he can accomplish with one touch what others need three or four touches to do. This will speed up his game.

Obviously, a coach can't expect matchlike performance if he's working with the youngest players. He must change his expectations. Instead of demanding a one-touch performance, he might merely confine the space in which they play. Then the youngsters will learn that in order to be successful, they have to get rid of the ball more quickly. This, essentially, will accomplish the same end, but it won't be as demanding for their limited skills.

Space Limitation

Space controls another progression. An exercise done in an unlimited space is much easier, and therefore less matchlike, than one where the space is confined.

No Limits:	No Pressure
Limits:	Limited Pressure
Confined Area:	Match Pressure

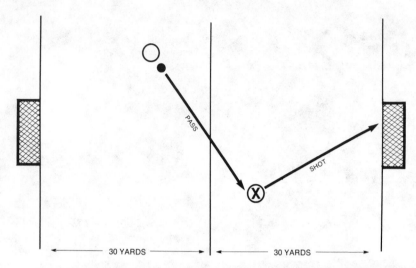

In a small-sided game, play becomes intensified by moving the goals closer to each other. If the offense gets the ball at the halfway line, they can't score, so there is relatively little defending pressure, and therefore very little offensive pressure. However, playing on goals that are closer to each other means that a possible shot is only one pass away. The players can finish in one pass, and the danger of scoring keeps the defenders very alert.

This progression can often be used in conjunction with the previous one. Once the players have mastered the one-touch skills, the coach should just make the field smaller. Or he can demand right foot only, left foot only, inside the foot only, or instep only, so that the exercise becomes even more difficult. We can push an exercise a little bit more and a little bit more all the time.

Addition of Goal

Finally, where the exercise is played will make a difference. An exercise performed in an isolated way is the least effective and least matchlike. Putting a goal at the end of the exercise adds more pressure, and if one or more defenders are placed in front of that goal, then we again have matchlike conditions.

Another good example of this progression is keep away, a game in which the object is to keep possession of the ball. If there is an extra

No Goal:	No Pressure
Goal:	Limited Pressure
Goal With Defense:	Match Pressure

players or two extra players on the side with the ball, then it is a picnic. The overload allows the player to take his time, and it gives him more opportunity to find an open player. However, if Keep Away is played with even numbers, it becomes very, very demanding, both physically and technically, and some pretty hard sprinting is needed in order to keep possession of the ball.

Training for Different Goals and Different Levels

By changing the progressions, a coach can use a particular exercise to train for different reasons. If he wanted to put top priority on fitness, he could introduce the exercise in a large area. If players had to go one-on-one over the whole field, they would be exhausted, and they probably wouldn't even get to the other goal. But if a coach does the exercise in a very tight space, he is putting a great deal of emphasis on skill. How good are the players in a confined area? How much room do they need to play this game?

This proves that it is ridiculous for anyone to believe that there are specific fitness exercises and specific skill exercises. In the barest sense, a coach needs no more than a few exercises to get all his goals accomplished. It is really only necessary to have variety because a coach must hold the players' interest and make it all less boring.

In the beginning, I mentioned that the exercises in this book can be used for anyone, from age five to age fifty, no matter what their skill level. The progression that I've tried to impart is the method that is used to step up the pace from an ordinary exercise that is appropriate for a seven-year-old to one that is challenging on the professional level. But it is still the same exercise.

We are always dealing with an essential element that belongs to the game. The professionals really do it no differently. The same tactics exist no matter who is playing, because, in the end, everybody is just playing soccer. They always have the basic nature of the game itself to contend with.

III. Warm-Up

Philosophy

A warm-up is absolutely necessary before any soccer should be played. Many players believe that if they just stretch a little, they will be fine and can get on with playing soccer. That is hardly the case. Cold muscles shouldn't be stretched; they have to be warmed up first. It is vital to do at the very least a little jogging or perhaps a few jumping jacks before any stretching is done. Then, only when the muscles have been used, can the stretching begin.

The exercises found in this chapter are forms of stretching and warming up that I like to call "ball gymnastics." Through ball gymnastics a player can get all types of stretching done in addition to acquiring ball experience, mobility, and a flexibility that reflects on all parts of the body. Whether a coach uses these exercises or the more traditional method of warming up, using light jogging and stretching, is not that important—*as long as the players warm up and stretch before every practice and game.* However, the advantage of ball gymnastics is that when a player uses the ball while warming up and stretching, in a sense he is also warming up mentally as well as physically.

Many of these exercises involve fitness and also involve the soccer ball, but don't have any direct relation to the way the soccer ball is used in a game. This is fine. Any contact with *any* ball is helpful. As I said before, youngsters who play other sports will surely have an advantage when they play soccer, because the first step for a young athlete is to develop eye/hand and eye/foot coordination. Any sport can do that. Any use of the soccer ball can do that too.

One-Person Warm-Ups

Bouncing the Ball

This is similar to dribbling with the basketball. Each player takes a ball and bounces it with his left hand, then with his right hand, and then with both hands as he slowly jogs around the field. Remember,

FIG. 3-1 *Players bouncing ball for warm-up.*

FIG. 3-2 *Players leaping in the air and catching the ball.*

FIG. 3-3 *End position for crunch. To start, player lies flat on his back.*

the point of this is to give the youngster a feel for the ball while doing the necessary activity to get his muscles warm.

Jumping for the Ball

The player should bounce the ball hard off the ground so that it flies high in the air—or if he can't get a high enough bounce, he should toss it into the air—and then leap off the ground to catch it, much in the same way that a goalkeeper would. Timing is vital in soccer and this exercise will develop it. Often the timing needed to leap and catch the ball is the same timing needed to leap and head the ball.

Crunches

The crunch is a sit-up exercise, where the player puts a ball between his feet, brings his legs in with knees bent and tries to touch the ball with his head.

Rocking

The player lies on his stomach and stiffens his body with his feet and shoulders off the ground. Now he rocks back and forth on his

FIG. 3-4A&B *Rocking on the stomach.*

FIG. 3-5 *Stomach dribbling.*

stomach. When a player lies on his stomach, he exercises his back, and when he lies on his back, he exercises his stomach.

Stomach Dribbling

Another exercise that will warm up the back muscles involves the same position. Again, the player is on his stomach with his feet and shoulders raised. Now he must hold this position and bounce a ball with his hand.

Push-Ups

The player should position himself as if he were going to do a normal push-up. However, this time, his hands should be on the ball instead of on the ground.

Body Bridge

In this exercise, the player lies flat on his back. He should have a ball in his hands, and his hands should be over his hips. Now he should take this ball and roll it across his body and then underneath his hips and out the other side and around again. He should do this several times in one direction and several times in the other direction.

FIG. 3-6A&B *Push-up on the ball.*

FIG. 3-7 Body bridge

Juggling

When one person is all by himself, juggling is one of the best warm-ups. The player should try to keep the ball up in the air, using his feet, thighs, or head. When lots of youngsters are juggling together, it is good to make a game out of it by suggesting a competition to get the most touches before the ball hits the ground. Juggling is not only a great way for a player to warm up, but a great way for him to get a good feel for how the ball responds to his touch.

Two-Person Warm-Ups

Sit-Up Exchange

The two players should sit feet to feet with their knees bent, and lock their ankles. Then they both lie flat on their backs. One player will have the ball. Now, when they sit up, the player with the ball passes it to his partner.

Leg Push

This is another exercise to strengthen the stomach. One player is standing. The other should lie on his back and grab his partner's

FIG. 3-8A *Juggling with thigh.*   **FIG. 3-8B** *Juggling with instep.*

ankles. The player on the ground raises his legs and his partner then pushes them gently to get them back on the ground. The player whose legs are being pushed must keep them straight and try not to let them touch the ground.

Over-Under Exchange

The two players are back to back again, now about two feet apart. They both lean back as far as they can, and the player with the ball passes it over the top to his partner. Now the two players bend over and pass the ball through their legs to each other. The exchange continues in this circular manner.

Figure Eight Exchange

Two players stand back to back about a foot apart. One player has the ball and twists to his right, keeping his feet stationary. The player behind him also twists to his right, which means they are still facing in opposite directions. The player with the ball hands it behind his back to the player without the ball. Now they both twist to the left and exchange the ball again. This continues in a figure eight pattern.

FIG. 3-9A&B *Sit-up exchange.*

FIG. 3-10 *Leg push.*

FIG. 3-11A *Over-under exchange—ball transferred over the head.*

FIG. 3-11B *Ball transferred under.*

FIG. 3-12 *Figure eight.*

Stomach Throw

The two players lie on their stomachs about five yards apart and throw the ball back and forth to each other, making sure they keep both their feet and their shoulders off the ground.

Warm-Up Games

Most of these games are done in the form of relay races, and not all of them use the ball. In general, though, they are still a mix between warming up, developing strength and general fitness, and working with the ball. Relays are a great gimmick to use with the very youngest players (although that's not to say that the older players don't like them as well) because in order to maintain some semblance of order, a coach has to make a game out of everything. This way the youngsters are competing; they don't know that they are also running and stretching. The worst thing a coach can do at that age is to lose the youngsters' attention.

Leapfrog

This children's game should be pretty familiar to everyone. In the most simple form, one player crouches down and the other player

FIG. 3-13 Stomach throw.

FIG. 3-14A Leapfrog.

FIG. 3-14B Crawling through partner's legs.

FIG. 3-15A *Relay race of leapfrog in a line.*

FIG. 3-15B *Relay race of alternating leapfrog and crawling.*

FIG. 3-16A Ball under legs.

FIG. 3-16C Ball over head.

FIG. 3-16B Sprint to the front.

FIG. 3-16D Alternating over and under.

leaps over him. Then the leaping player crouches down and his partner jumps over him. To vary this game, a coach can have the players leap over each other and then crawl through each other's legs.

To make it more of a traditional relay race, a coach can line up many leaping posts, and after a player goes through the line, he becomes the final post at the end. Meanwhile, the next person in line is going through the posts. Once all the players have gone through, the team has finished. The coach can again have the players alternate between over and under.

Under-Over Exchange

The players should line up about two feet apart, one behind the other. The person in the front has the ball. He must pass it *under* (or through) his legs to the person behind him. That person then passes it through his legs to the person behind him, and so on. When the ball reaches the end of the line, the last player sprints to the front and starts it again. This time, however, the players pass the ball over their heads. Again, when it gets to the end of the line, the last player sprints forward with it. Now the ball is passed back, alternating over and under.

Running Races

All-out sprinting is great for the players because they really need to be in shape to play soccer, but all-out sprinting is just plain boring. A coach can spice it up a bit by including the ball. He can have a dribbling race.

He can have the players carry the ball under the arm while they run.

He can have them roll the ball along the ground with their hands as they run.

Wheelbarrow

Wheelbarrow is about as well known as leapfrog, so there is no need to go into much detail about it. One player stands up and lifts his partner's ankles off the ground. The partner now is on his hands and must walk on them.

Piggyback

Piggyback rides (one player on the back of another) are excellent fitness vehicles (no pun intended). The exercise strengthens both arms and legs, and if the players run while they are giving the ride, it

FIG. 3-17 Dribbling relay race.

FIG. 3-18 Carrying the ball in a race.

FIG. 3-19 *Rolling the ball in a race.*

FIG. 3-20 *Wheelbarrow race.*

FIG. 3-21 *Piggyback race.*

develops endurance. A coach can combine these last two exercises by having the pair wheelbarrow to one end and piggyback to the other. He should just make sure that the one who walks on his hands is the one who gets to ride on the way back.

Dead Man

One player stands in the middle as stiffly as possible. The other players sit around him with their feet meeting his feet. Then they push the player back and forth between them. This is a good strength exercise and one that the youngsters love to do.

Circuit Training

All these ball gymnastics could be combined into something called *circuit training.* A coach should have a general fitness circuit—where the players really get a tough physical workout—and a soccer exercise circuit—where the players work on technical skills. Circuit training involves setting up what is essentially a course, with ten or eleven warm-up stations. Every station is a different exercise, and the players spend one minute doing each exercise. They do not all start in the same place but, rather, are spread out at the different

FIG. 3-22 *Dead man in the middle.*

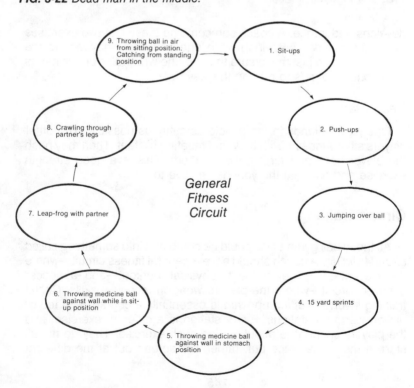

General Fitness Circuit

1. Sit-ups

2. Push-ups

3. Jumping over ball

4. 15 yard sprints

5. Throwing medicine ball against wall in stomach position

6. Throwing medicine ball against wall while in sit-up position

7. Leap-frog with partner

8. Crawling through partner's legs

9. Throwing ball in air from sitting position. Catching from standing position

stations. The coach should time a one minute rest after each workout and then move the players on to the next station.

General Fitness Circuit

Players should pair up. One player works out for up to one minute and the other player rests. (The length of time may change depending on age or level of demand.) Then they switch. After both have done the prescribed exercise, they move to the next station. The resting player should have a scorecard to keep track of the number of repetitions. The coach should allow only ten seconds to move between stations.

Soccer Style Circuit

In this circuit, both players work at the same time, sometimes individually and sometimes together, for one minute. Then, after a one or two minute rest, they move on to the next station. (Work and rest time is flexible, depending on age or what we want to accomplish.)

IV. Passing

The Many Types of Passing

Passing is the essence of soccer. It is far easier for a player to move the ball forward, to throw his opponent off guard, and to set up a beautiful shot if he knows how to pass well. There are so many ways, physically, to pass—short kicks, long kicks, chips, volleys, half volleys, headers—and there are so many reasons, strategically, why passing is so important.

The Inside of the Foot

A simple short pass is usually done with the inside of the foot. In order to do this a player's toe must come up, the ankle must be locked, and the ball must be struck with the inside of the foot.

The Instep

More effective than the inside of the foot is the instep pass. This is almost always used for a longer pass and can even be used for shorter ones. The instep is located on the top of the foot where the shoelaces are. This area is the most rigid part of the foot. A player simply needs to feel the bone in that area to confirm the fact that there is no "give" to it. If a player hits the ball with his instep, therefore, his full power will go into the shot. Moving away from the instep there will be less than maximal power.

The Inside of the Instep

Then we have the *inside* of the instep (which gives the ball a spin). The reason we consider it one of the instep kicks rather than an inside kick is because of the toe position. Instead of the toe being up, it is pointed down. However, we are not doing a straight kick anymore. We are coming around a bit, and putting a spin on it. In a *clean* instep kick, the ball will not spin.

FIG. 4-1 *Inside of the foot.*

FIG. 4-2 *The instep.*

FIG. 4-3 *The inside of the instep.*

The Outside of the Instep

Then we have the *outside* of the instep. The toe must be pointed inside, and the kick is done with the outside.

The Volley

Volleys should be fired directly off the instep of the foot. The player brings his knee up and points his toes down. A good way for a youngster to learn the volley is to have him kick the ball out of his hands against a wall. It should come back in the air, and the player can catch it and do it again. This is often a good skill to learn even before ground passes, because it forces the youngster to use his instep to kick.

Often, young players have a tough time locating their instep, so they will use their toes or the inside of their feet. Older players may have trouble kicking the ball with their instep without catching their foot on the ground. Little kids do have an advantage in that respect because their feet are usually fairly small and the ball is big in comparison. They rarely have to worry about catching their feet. Yet still they do not like to use the instep. In the volley, however, there is almost no other way to kick.

FIG. 4-4 The outside of the instep.

FIG. 4-5A To practice the volley, the ball can be dropped from the hands.

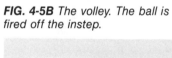

FIG. 4-5B The volley. The ball is fired off the instep.

The Half Volley

As we now have a good feel for the volley in the air, we then try to drop kick, with the half volley. This means that the kicker lets the ball drop and as it hits the ground, it will bounce back up—and in that split second the player should kick. This eliminates the danger of catching the toe on the ground and the player, once he gets his timing right, can have a good, clean instep kick.

One-Person Passing Exercises

The Ball Net

Believe it or not, there are several good ways to practice passing skills without another person. An excellent way to introduce a good feel for the instep kick is to put the ball in a small ball net or on a rope. The player can hold either the net or the rope in his hands, and as he walks along, he can kick the ball with his instep. He could go shopping this way. In many other parts of the world, this is a very common practice. It is not unusual to see a kid coming down the road

FIG. 4-6 *The half-volley. The ball is still fired off the instep but it hits the ground first.*

FIG. 4-7 *The ball net.*

FIG. 4-8A&B *Passing against a wall.*

with his ball net in his hand, kicking the ball with each step he takes. It's an excellent way to get the proper feel, because it is obvious when the ball has been caught well. That feeling comes very quickly.

Passing against a Wall

A wall is probably more effective as a passing aid than another player. A youngster can spend hours with a wall, trying different passes, such as short kicks, long kicks, kicks with the right foot, kicks with the left foot, one touch, two touch, chipping (kicking the ball into the air), volleys, half volleys, and combinations of these (left foot, short kick, two touch, for example), and the wall will always return the ball to him. Beginners—until they have control of the ball—should only worry about controlling the ball before they kick it back, and not concern themselves at this point with the one-touch or two-touch kicks.

Two-Person Passing Exercises

Passing between Two People

When another person is added, it is essentially the same thing. They use the same variety of passes and the same foot motion, but now they just eliminate the wall. The two players should progress from the very simplest of passes to the more complicated for at least two reasons. First, it is always better to warm up before attempting any long kicks—otherwise, a player might end up with a pulled muscle—and second, the skills that are more difficult to master will seem easier if the player has already gotten a feel for the ball.

Playing the Ball into a Space

This progression fits in nicely here. The previous exercise mentioned that the players should progress from the most simple technique for passing to the most demanding. The next two exercises will use the same drill, but with a progression in the level of intensity.

The two players begin with simple passing back and forth; any type of passing is acceptable. Then, once this skill is mastered, the players begin to move and cut for the ball. The passing player should not hit it directly to the receiving player; instead, he should force the receiving player to run for the ball, bringing the play closer to matchlike conditions.

FIG. 4-9 *Passing between two people.*

FIG. 4-10 *Players passing and moving.*

Power Passing

After the two players have done this for a while, they should come in a little closer to one another, maybe about fifteen to twenty yards apart, depending on the age, and pass the ball as hard as possible. It doesn't matter if the ball hits the receiving player on the chest or the thigh or the foot, or wherever. As long as the passing player hits him, that's what the receiver has to deal with. He must settle the ball, bring it under control, and then give the same hard kick back to his partner. The passer can serve as hard a ball as he wants to, but he has to hit the receiver. This provides target-shooting practice as well as skill in bringing a ball under control.

It is easy to see how this drill, the most basic one that we know, becomes a professional exercise. It is still two people passing the ball back and forth to one another, but there has been a change in philosophy. Not all balls in a match come gently. A player may be fed the most extreme ones and should still manage to cope with them. That is why practice should often be that way, too. The level of toughness must continually increase for a player to become a master of the ball.

FIG. 4-11 *Passing through cones for accuracy.*

Passing through Cones

If the players are having trouble making accurate passes, a coach may want to set up two sets of cones about twenty yards apart. The cones in each set should be about two yards apart. A player should be behind each set of cones.

These two players pass back and forth, and the primary goal is to get the ball through both sets of cones. By placing the cones at least twenty yards apart (a shorter distance for the younger players because they don't always have the strength to kick the ball that far), the coach is forcing the players to use their insteps to pass; otherwise they would not have enough power to get the ball that distance. This is the type of pass where accuracy is more likely to be a problem. Usually, the inside of the foot is pretty accurate.

Running in an Arc

In this exercise, one person, the server, will be passing normally. The other person, the runner, will be trying to hook his passes back to the server on both the left and the right sides. We are now working on cutting around the ball, which happens so many times in a game. It is especially good for situations when the ball gets near the touch line and the player must hook it back into the field to keep it from going out. This also teaches the players that they must go after the ball. They should not wait for it to come to them.

The server remains relatively stationary and passes the ball at an angle to one side of his partner. That person should sprint to the ball and, we hope, with one touch hook the ball back to the feet of the server. Now the server will pass it to the other side, and the same thing happens in reverse. The running player will essentially be moving in an arc across the playing area. He must also keep a close distance, because if he moves farther back or it becomes a simple drill, the challenge is gone. Once the players get used to this exercise, the server should stop alternating left and right and start trying to fool the receiver. The receiver could already be halfway over to the left because he just got a pass from the right—and then the server hits it back to the right again. But the server cannot put the ball out of reach.

Side Volley

If a coach is looking for a variation on the previous exercise, he can have the server throw balls for a volley, instead of passing the balls on the ground. (The coach may also have the server throw balls for head shots, but that is discussed in Chapter VI on heading.) The server should throw the ball in the air; without letting it touch the

FIG. 4-12A *Player receives the ball on his left.*

FIG. 4-12B *Player receives the ball on his right.*

FIG. 4-13A *Player volleys the ball back with left foot.*

FIG. 4-13B *Player volleys the ball back with his right foot.*

ground, the player must kick the ball with his instep back into the server's hands. If the coach is working with the younger kids, he should have them stand still and do this until they have mastered the skill of volleying. Once they have, however, the runner should be moving to the right or the left, depending on where the ball is served.

Running Backward

The server and his partner should be about five yards apart, facing each other. As the server moves forward, his partner moves backward. As I've said before, any kind of moving and running is better than practicing a skill in a stationary position. The server tosses the ball to his partner, who then volleys it back into the server's hands. A variation on this drill with an emphasis on the receiving end is included later in this chapter.

Three-Person Passing Exercises

The Weave

The weave is a somewhat intricate passing exercise that works on the same principles as the exercise we just described. It may also be

FIG. 4-14 *Passing while jogging backward.*

called follow-the-ball, and it helps the youngsters develop some basic tactical skills in addition to the more obvious passing skills.

Three players stand facing the field, about fifteen yards apart from on another. The middle player (square) has the ball. He passes it to his left (or his right-it's not important, but we will start with his left for the example) and then proceeds to follow in that direction. He runs *behind* the left-hand player (diamond) who is moving to meet the ball. At the same time, the right-hand player (triangle) runs forward to prepare to receive a pass from the left-hand player. Now the player with the ball (diamond) passes to the right and then follows his pass over to the right, again running *behind* the receiving player. This receiving player (triangle) picks up the ball and passes it to his left to the first player (square), who has been running forward in anticipation of receiving the pass.

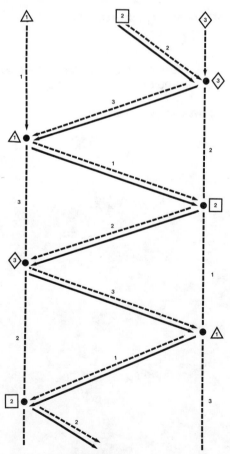

(Legend for Diagrams is in Appendix.)

This weaving in and out continues all the way down the field, where it will end with a shot on goal. It is an excellent exercise for helping the youngsters move to the ball and fill in the open spaces.

Short-Short-Long

The three players should stand in a line about fifteen or twenty yards apart from one another. The ball should start on the end. This end person passes it to the player in the middle. The middle player then passes the ball back to the person he received it from. Now this end person makes a long chip pass to the player on the other end. This third player passes the ball into the middle, where the middle person will have turned around to receive the ball. The play continues in this short-short-long fashion. If possible, this should all be done as one-touch passing, certainly no more than two-touch passing.

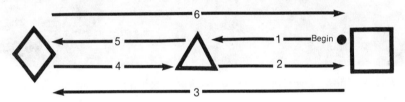

Two Balls

Still using this same format—three people in a line—the coach can now add two balls. Each person on the end has a ball and the purpose of this drill is to give the center person a real workout. It is good to do this one on a timed basis: one minute in the middle, then the players switch positions.

The middle player receives the ball from one end and passes it back immediately. As soon as the player on the other end sees the middle player return the pass, he should serve the ball. If he times it correctly, it should just be reaching the middle player as he turns around. The middle player now passes that ball back and turns to find yet another ball coming at him from the other direction.

Combination

Believe it or not, there is an exercise that forces the middle player to work even harder! Now one of the servers passes the ball to the middle player's feet for a foot pass back, and the other server tosses it to his head for a head pass back. The middle player must work like crazy to keep up and get the balls back with good passes.

FIG. 4-15A&B *Player receives the ball from each end in rapid succession.*

FIG. 4-16A *Player passes with feet.*

FIG. 4-16B *Player passes with head.*

Aside from the obvious conditioning benefits of this type of exercise, it is important to provide situations where the player is under so much pressure jumping and flying and running that there is no time for him to think about the actual skills involved. These skills have to become as natural as breathing, and the only way to test this is to create a situation that allows the player no time to think, because that is what it will be like, come match time.

If a player can deal with a situation like this in practice, it will prepare him better for the fast pace and confusion that will hit him in the game itself. In fact, after an exercise like this one, the game may even seem a little easy. Isn't that a much better position to be in than the opposite one? If the skills are practiced only in low-key situations during the training session, then the actual game will seem much more difficult. That is not to say that a coach shouldn't begin work on a skill in a simplified manner, but he should always move from the comfortable situation to an outright nasty one. We hope, the player's skills will also move and grow with this progression.

Heel Pass

The exercise should be set up as a takeover situation. One player should begin running down the field with the ball. A teammate and a

FIG. 4-17 *Heel pass by stepping on the ball.*

FIG. 4-18 *Heel pass using the opposite foot.*

FIG. 4-19 *Heel pass using the backswing.*

defender should approach him from the other direction. As the defender attacks, the player with the ball makes a heel pass back to his teammate. There are several types of heel passes that a player can use. He can step lightly on top of the ball and roll it backward with the sole of his foot.

He can step over the ball, and before his foot hits the ground, use the momentum of the backswing to hit the ball.

Finally, he can step over with one foot and kick with the other.

Four- (or More) Person Passing Exercises

Line Passing

This exercise works especially well if the players have mastered the skill of one-touch passing. Four or more players are needed for this (although if there are more than eight, it might be better to divide the group into two sets of lines). Two lines form, with the players behind one another, and stand opposite each other. There should be one ball. The first player in one line passes to the first player in the other line, then runs to the end of the opposite line. This goes on in an endless cycle.

FIG. 4-20 *Line passing.*

Wall Passes or Give and Go

The coach should designate some people (the squares in Fig. 4) to be the "walls" or stations. They are spread out all over the field. The other players (triangles) each have a ball and run in any direction. Whenever they can, they pass to one of the stationary people. Then, instead of just standing while they wait for the return ball, they should continue moving, the way they would in an actual game. The stationary player passes the ball back, leading the moving player slightly. The moving player then looks for the next open station.

This teaches players to move and look and pass, all at the same time. They have to be looking for the open spaces to move into. There might be a time when they have to carry the ball if a station isn't available. They also have to be alert and anticipate when someone else might be passing a ball to that station. This is comparable to being alert in a game and knowing when someone is available to receive a pass.

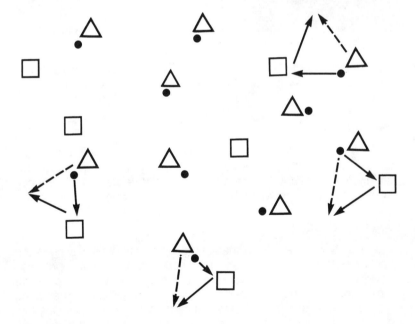

Receiving

Receiving, or trapping the ball, doesn't necessarily have to be separated from passing because the skills have to be used at the same time. However, there are some exercises that stress the

FIG. 4-21 *Receiving the ball.*

receiving end particularly. For instance, passing work on the wall can be used to stress the receiving end if a player pays attention to settling the ball carefully each time it comes back to him.

Tossing the Ball

When a player does not have a wall, he can throw the ball up in the air and trap it with various parts of his body. This helps to get his timing down straight. If the timing isn't right, the ball will just bounce away—instead of being cushioned—and will become a loose ball.

Running Backward

The only other exercise that will focus purely on receiving is the one where a server and a receiver, about five yards apart, progress down the field. While the receiver is running backward the server throws the ball to his head and the receiver heads it back. After doing this a specified number of times, the server throws the ball to the feet of the receiver, who passes it back and continues running backward. Finally, the server either passes or throws the ball to different parts of the receiver's body. No matter where the ball comes, the receiver should bring it under control, drop it to his feet, and continue running backward.

The server then runs up to the ball and serves it again.

FIG. 4-22A *Server and receiver.*

FIG. 4-22B *Chest trap.*

FIG. 4-22C *Thigh trap.*

FIG. 4-22D *Foot trap.*

V. Dribbling

Two Basic Elements

Touching the ball in any direction, moving the ball, being prepared to cut to the left or to the right, hooking it backward in order to evade a defender, or stopping and starting are really what dribbling is all about. Dribbling certainly is never just in one direction—it's in any direction, depending on how things close down or open up.

There are two ways of focusing on dribbling skills, and exercises for both are included here. The first consists mostly of what was described in the previous paragraph, going against a defender, one-on-one, and finding a way to get past him. The second is moving forward, trying to push the ball down the field, which uses dribbling less as a way to evade and more as a way to carry the ball forward.

This latter type of dribbling consists essentially of moving and sprinting while still keeping the ball under control. It means that the player always stays close enough to the ball to be able to play it off to someone else if he has to. The distance may vary depending on the exact situation, but the player's ability to have the ball under his control is the key element. Every time it gets away, it becomes a loose ball situation.

Players often think that the more speed they have, the better off they will be. They kick the ball way out in front of them, thinking that they will get to the goal faster if they don't touch the ball with their foot on every step. But the minute the ball gets too far out in front of them, they no longer have any control, and it might be stolen easily. If the player wants to add some speed to his play, he should not sacrifice control. That is primary.

The only situation where a player can safely put the ball out of quick reach is in a breakaway situation where there is a lot of space. Essentially, he is still in control because there are no defenders in the immediate area who can get to the ball first. But still the dribbler must have a feel for just how far ahead he can put the ball. The ball will be rolling toward the goalie or defensemen and away from the dribbler, so the situation is slightly more complicated than it seems.

The length and style of the dribble really depend on the situation; control is mandatory throughout.

Creative Dribbling

Practicing Alone

Dribbling is the simplest skill for a player to practice by himself. All he needs is a ball. A wide open space isn't even necessary. With the ball, the player should practice moving backward and forward and to the right and to the left. He should practice touching the ball to move it or dragging the ball to move it. Trees, lawn chairs, fire hydrants, and so on can all be make-believe defenders that he must fake out and evade. A little practice in his free time is an excellent way for a player to get the proper feel for the ball and how he can control it.

Dribbling in the Penalty Box

For this exercise, the players should all be scattered throughout the penalty box, and each one should have a ball. All the players have to do is run around with the ball, but as they run around in the box, they are supposed to practice dribbling techniques and looking up for other players so that they don't run into each other. Once the youngsters get the feel for this type of confined dribbling, the coach

FIG. 5-1 Dribbling in the penalty box. Every player has a ball.

can shout out suggestions like "Find open space to run into" or "Use both feet" or "Cut to the right" or "Cut to the left." These commands can be anything that will make the players think and use a change-up.

Fitness in the Penalty Box

Then the coach could have the players stop dribbling, and turn the exercise into one for fitness. Each player puts the ball out in front of him and hops up and down, touching the ball with alternating feet. Then, still using this hopping style, players should try to move the balls around the box.

Eliminate the Balls

One modification to this exercise turns the drill into a game. This is a great way to entertain the youngest players. As they are dribbling, the players try to eliminate one another from the penalty box by kicking one of the other players' balls out beyond the boundaries of

FIG. 5-2 *Dribbling becomes a contest. The players try to eliminate each other's balls.*

the box. Once a player's ball has been kicked out of the box he must leave the box. (It is a good idea to have him do toe touches or juggle on the outside so that he is not just standing there.) The player who is able to defend his ball to the end, while everyone else's balls are kicked out in turn, is the winner. This will help a player learn to protect and shield the ball from defenders while he is dribbling. This is an important skill to have.

Relay Races

A coach can create all types of relay races to emphasize these creative dribbling skills. All he has to do is to pick out one skill—say, for example, dragging the ball with the sole of the foot—and set it up in a relay-race situation. This is a great way to teach these skills to the youngest players. Other skills the coach can use include straight dribbling, left-foot-only dribbling, backward dribbling, and weaving in and out of cones.

FIG. 5-3A *Relay race—dragging the ball with the sole of the foot.*

FIG. 5-3B *Relay race—dribbling through a slalom course.*

Dribbling to Move the Ball Down the Field

Sprinting Around Cones

Two cones should be set up about fifteen to twenty yards apart. The player must dribble as fast as he can from the first cone to the second, then turn around the far cone and slowly dribble back. The change-up in speed parallels the dribbling in a game, where a player must learn to slow down or speed up the ball, depending on what the situation demands. This exercise, however, should place an emphasis on speed, with the player always remembering to keep the ball under control.

It is important to make sure the distance between the cones is about fifteen to twenty yards. It gives the players enough space to pick up speed, but not so much that they can let the ball get far ahead of them and not keep it in control.

Dribbling on Goal

For this exercise, the coach should put a marker about twenty to thirty yards from the goal. The actual distance will depend on the age and strength of the players. They should have a marker, essentially,

FIG. 5-4 *Sprinting around cones.*

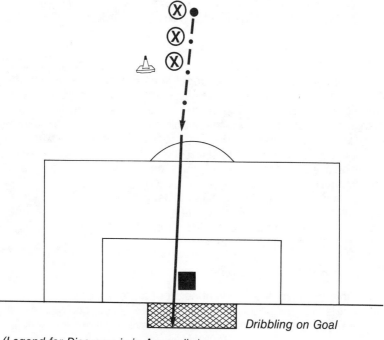

Dribbling on Goal

(Legend for Diagrams is in Appendix.)

so that they don't drift forward and begin to dribble five yards from the goal. This won't give anyone real practice.

Each player starts with the ball behind the marker and dribbles in as if it were a breakaway situation. When the player reaches shooting range, he should take the shot. The goalkeeper should feel free, and actually be encouraged, to come out of the goal to get any ball that a dribbler has allowed to become loose.

One-on-One on Goal

We can build this up closer to matchlike conditions by adding a defender. Now the player either has to shoot earlier or use a creative dribbling tactic to get by the defender.

The number of people lining up behind the cone should not create a situation where there are more people standing than working. By the time the player takes a shot and gets back in line, he should almost be able to go again. If that is not the case, then the exercise becomes one of standing in line. (This drill should certainly not be done if there's only one ball in a practice session, because it just becomes a waste of time for everyone there.)

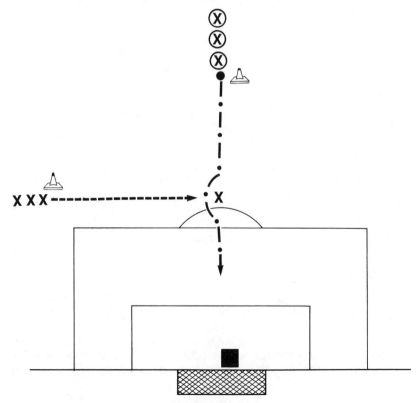

Dribbling with a Cross

This exercise is similar to the last one in that the dribbling effort ends with something else. In this case, it is a cross instead of a shot. Two lines should form back near the midfield. One line, near the touchline, will contain the dribblers. The first person in this line will dribble down the outside lane, while a player from the line in the center of the field, the shooters, runs parallel to him. When the dribbling player gets to the corner, he should cross the ball to the center of the field. Now the shooter must bring the ball under control and take a shot on goal.

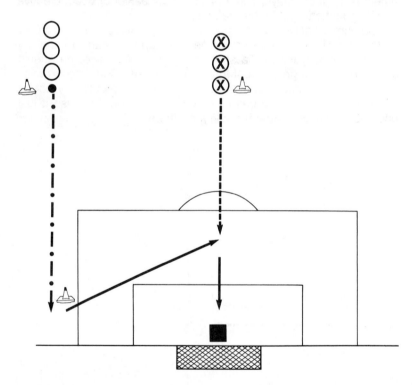

Crossing with a Defender

This exercise is identical to the last one, but now we are introducing a third line. This line is down by the goal and will be the defenders. When the dribbler and the shooter begin their runs, the defender moves out in front of the goal. This creates much more of a challenge for the shooter, who will often have to take the shot without settling the ball first. The coach should also point out the option of

FIG. 5-5 Dribbling to get by a defender.

heading the ball into the goal. Also, the dribbler may move the ball toward the goal before he crosses it, in hopes that the defenseman will move out to challenge him.

It is fairly easy to see the progression from simple to matchlike in these exercises. I hope coaches will begin to recognize the importance of this method in teaching soccer.

Slalom Course

Line up cones or players so that they are four or five steps away from each other. The dribbler should then proceed through this slalom course as fast as he can without losing the ball. If the coach decides to use players instead of cones, he can have the players play a slight defense—certainly not all out—to force the dribbler to protect the ball the way he would in a game. When the dribbler is done, he passes the ball to the front of the line and becomes the last post in the slalom course. The exercise repeats until everyone in the line has dribbled through. Obviously, this is a perfect exercise to use as a relay race, whether you use cones or players to mark the course.

What is always helpful in an exercise such as this one is to end up with a shot on goal. We should put the finishing end on a drill as often as we can. It prepares the players for what we really want to do: put the ball in the net.

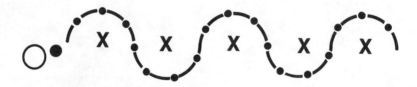

VI. Heading

Heading is one of the hardest skills to impart to youngsters, perhaps because they are not willing to sacrifice their head to hit the ball. The coaches should make sure that the balls are not too heavy or too hard. Young players are hesitant enough as it is, and if the heavy ball is going to hurt them, they will always shy away from heading. It is a very important part of the game, however, and it must be taught correctly to be effective.

In order to head the ball, the player must fix his neck, reach back, and then snap forward, striking the ball with his forehead. The power of heading will come from the stomach and back muscles. It is imperative that the player watch the ball all the time or else he will most likely receive it in the face.

Heading should be used for passing to another player or shooting on goal. It can be done standing still or moving, or the player may dive into it. No matter what, he still must fix his neck and keep a careful eye on the ball as it comes toward him. Unfortunately, the ball is not always going to be set up for the perfect header in a game. The ball could be glancing off any part of the head. If a youngster learns the essentials, though, the rest will come fairly easily.

One-Person Heading Exercises

Pendulum

A pendulum, otherwise known as a ball on a rope, is the best tool for learning heading skills. The player should hang the ball from a tree branch or a "T". The ball should be at forehead level, so that the player can get the feel of hitting the ball on his forehead. He does it softly at first, getting comfortable with the swing and the heading motion. Then he should increase his power. It will be very easy to see if the ball is hit correctly because it will swing directly back. If the ball is not hit properly, it will swing off to one side or jump around on the rope.

Once this skill is mastered, developing it is a simple matter of just raising the rope. Now the player must jump up to reach the ball. This forces him to bend his back and snap forward with his entire body. Again, it will be important to hit the ball head on or it will not come swinging back in a straight line.

FIG. 6-1AB&C *Proper heading form.*

FIG. 6-2A&B Using the pendulum in a standing position.

FIG. 6-3A&B The pendulum is raised and now the player must jump in order to reach the ball.

Then, even harder, the ball should be raised higher. Now the player must take a running start and leap for the ball. After he hits the ball and it is swinging wildly, he should do it again. He should not return the ball to the stationary position because this will never be the situation in a game. Not only will this running-start heading be the closest to a matchlike heading situation, but it will also help train the player physically by developing his leg muscles and his ability to jump.

Juggling

Juggling with the head is another way for a youngster to develop a feel for using his head to play soccer. It is not as good as the pendulum because it doesn't force the youngster to use the proper heading motion, but it is an exercise he can do alone—and anything that will get a player accustomed to playing the ball with his head is helpful.

FIG. 6-4 *The pendulum is even higher, forcing the player to take a running leap.*

FIG. 6-5A&B *Juggling with the head.*

Two-Person Heading Exercises

Server and Header

Two players stand no more than five to seven yards apart. One player is a server and the other player is a header. The server should throw underhand in order to ensure accuracy. They should start this in a stationary position, just to get the feel of it. Then, as they feel more comfortable with the motion, the ball should be thrown a little higher and the header should jump for it. Finally, the players should progress backward or forward across the field. It is very difficult to jog backward and jump up into the ball at the same time.

It is tough enough to get a youngster to use his head in a game, but it's nearly impossible to get him to do a diving header. Yet this is a very useful skill to have. In order to get the youngsters thinking along these lines, there is a special drill the coach can use. Again, there is a server and a header. This time the header is on the ground in a push-up position. When the server tosses the ball, the header pushes with his hands and his feet and actually leaps into the ball.

FIG. 6-6 *Server and header.*

FIG. 6-7A *Diving header can be practiced by starting in a push-up position.*

Moving in an Arc

Most of the heading exercises, including the one I'm about to describe, have also been mentioned in Chapter IV on passing; it is often a good idea to use these in the same training session, because the players will have already gotten a feel from the passing drill. This exercise, like the previous heading exercises, uses a header and a server. The server is stationary while the header moves back and forth in an arc, heading the ball back to the server each time.

Scoring with the Head

If the server stands near the goal, the players can learn how to use their heading skills to score goals. Balls are either thrown or crossed with the foot, then the heading player runs onto the ball and finishes on goal. If the players do this often enough, it might become second nature in a game, and that is what we are striving for. Repetition will make them master it.

FIG. 6-7B *Diving header.*

FIG. 6-8A&B *Approaching head shots from the left and right.*

FIG. 6-9 *Head shot on goal.*

Three-Person Heading Exercises

Blocking the Header

Two people stand about ten or fifteen feet apart. One is a server and the other is a header. A third person remains stationary right in front of the header, blocking him. The server should be throwing the ball just over the blocker's head. The header is forced to jump up in order to get to the ball. Later, when the youngsters are more used to this situation, the blocker jumps as well. Timing is important. Here we have another natural progression from the simple—a server and a header—to the most difficult and matchlike—heading from behind a moving opponent.

Juggling in a Group

A group of three or more is good for juggling practice. All the players have to do is to keep the ball up in the air, using their heads.

Two-Touch Juggling

An exercise for more advanced soccer players is two-touch juggling. The ball comes to the player, who, instead of hitting it back immediately, heads it up first in front of him and then back to the other

FIG. 6-10A Blocker in middle is stationary.

FIG. 6-10B Blocker actively tries to get the ball.

FIG. 6-10C *Blocker actively tries to get the ball.*

FIG. 6-11 *Juggling in a group.*

player. This is tough to do with the youngest kids because they just don't have the capabilities to make it work, but it is excellent practice for the older kids who need to master more advanced skills in order to become better players.

Short-Short-Long

Another tough exercise that should be reserved for the more advanced players is the short-short-long passing drill, only this time the players use their heads instead of their feet. The three people are in a line, each about five yards from the other, considerably closer than in the passing drill. The player in the middle receives the ball from the player on one end. He heads it back to the same player. That player then hits a long head shot over to the person on the far end. Meanwhile, the player in the middle has turned around and receives a short header from the player on the other end. This goes back and forth—short, short, long—without the ball ever touching the ground (we hope).

FIG. 6-12 Short-short-long using only head balls.

Backward Heading

There are two variations of this. One is to have the person in the middle head the ball backward instead of heading it back to the first server. In this case, all the head passes are short ones; we have eliminated the long pass and introduced backward heading instead.

Two Balls

The other option is to add another ball. This is, again, similar to a passing exercise we described earlier. The two end people alternate serving the ball to the middle person, while he turns and faces first one player and then the other. In this case, the header always heads the ball back to the player who served it to him.

Circle Heading

Any number of players can get together to practice their heading— and they should—by standing in a circle and trying to keep the ball in

FIG. 6-13 *Player in the middle receives the balls in rapid succession from left and right.*

the air. Ideally, there should be a number of people on the outside and a few people in the middle. It's not a game of Keep Away; this just gives everyone more options. The ball can be played to anyone, and this game can be played at any time. The players don't even need a large area to practice heading skills.

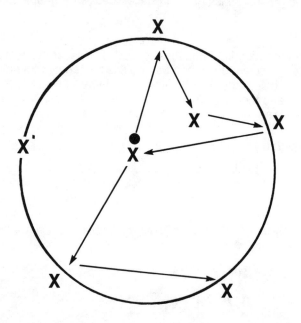

VII. Shooting

Shooting is primarily a variation on passing. It is most often done with the instep, although occasionally it is done with the inside of the foot. It all depends on the type of touch needed in the scoring situation. I like to compare shooting to passing because it clears up the misconception that a shot must be a rocket ball, hit so powerfully that it puts a hole in the back of the net. That is not always the answer. Sometimes a ball needs a delicate touch or a head shot or a chip just out of the goalie's reach. Because of this, it might be more accurate to refer to shooting as *finishing*. A shot on goal finishes the sequences of passes and maneuvers that brought the ball down the field.

However, there is one major difference between shooting and passing. The player is no longer trying to get a ball *to* a person; now he is trying to get the ball *by* a person, namely, the goalkeeper. Passing means that the ball is supposed to reach somebody, whether it be at their feet or in a space where the person can run onto it. When we pass we have to do it in a manner that makes it receivable, but when we shoot, this is the last thing we want. In a shooting situation, it is the net and not a teammate that is doing all the receiving. Shooting involves a different type of striking from both the physical and mental standpoints.

I want to emphasize the mental aspect. We have to know how to catch the keeper off balance. The player must be aware of where the keeper is, where he can get to, and where he cannot get to. A player who has a hard shot will do his team no good if he hits it to the keeper's hands every time. This is another reason why I use the word *finishing:* the word *shooting* immediately makes everyone think of the physical act, while finishing combines both the physical and the mental aspects. Finishing is, for the most part, a beat-the-keeper deal rather than a hit at full force. Of course, a shot at full force certainly is one possibility for beating the keeper, but finishing encompasses a lot more.

In shooting, the planting foot is important too, because its placement provides timing, balance, and control. The position of the planting foot has a lot to do with whether the ball will rise or stay low.

One-Person Shooting Exercises

Against the Wall

If a player is all by himself, it is much better to practice shooting against a wall than on the goal. One simple reason is that the ball will

FIG. 7-1 *The position of the planting foot should be taken into consideration.*

FIG. 7-2AB&C *Shooting at a target on the wall.*

come back to him instead of getting stuck in the net; this means more practice time. The main advantage, however, is that the player can now set up targets. He can mark an area on the wall, or pick an obvious target, and then take shot after shot, trying to hit that spot. Target shooting is far more helpful than random shooting. The player should change his target frequently, making sure he uses both ground shots and shots in the air. He should try to do volleys, half volleys, headers, and chips, and he should take shots with the inside, outside, and instep of his foot. As a final variation he should alternate using his left foot and his right foot.

At a Goal

If a player does not have a wall but he does have a goal, then he should announce to himself where he is going to place each ball before he takes the shot. For example, he could say, "Upper left corner" and then do his best to place the ball there. Or he could say "In the middle, on the ground," and try for that area. It is very important for a player to think about where he wants to put a shot.

Two-Person Shooting Exercises

Shooting from a Cross

With two players, we can now introduce shooting from a pass or a cross. The player should put the ball into the goal with one touch. While this is considerably more difficult than one person shooting by himself, it is a far more common situation in a game. As a result, when two players are together, it is good to introduce a serving player who will pass the ball or cross it from the touchline to the shooting

(Legend for Diagrams is in Appendix.)

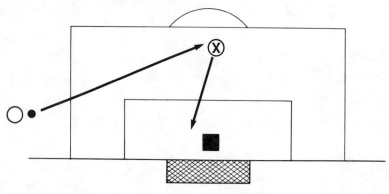

player. The server should pass the ball in from all sides. Then the two players switch positions. Even though there is considerably less time to think and plan in this exercise, it is still very important for the shooter to be aware of the goalkeeper and where he wants to place the ball. This is also an excellent way to practice head shots on goal.

Starting with the Back toward the Goal

A similar exercise would entail placing the shooter in front of the goal with his back to the goal. A server stands thirty to thirty-five yards from the goal (closer if the server is a youngster) and passes the ball in a variety of ways to the shooter. The shooter, who is now receiving with his back to the goal, settles it, turns, and shoots. This drill should start off with no defense, but then as it progresses, and if there are more players, the coach can put a defender in, and then maybe another shooter, and then another defender.

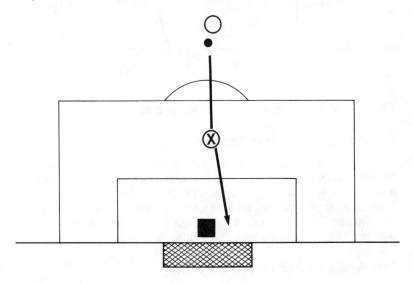

Wall Pass Shots

Incorporating a wall pass into the shooting exercise adds yet another element. Essentially, the server and the shooter are in the opposite positions from the last drill. The server stands with his back to the goal and the shooter dribbles toward him. The shooter should then pass to the server and cut either to the left or to the right (the coach should make sure they practice both because most kids will always cut to the side of their dominant foot), and the server will pass the ball in that direction. Then it is just a matter of taking a shot.

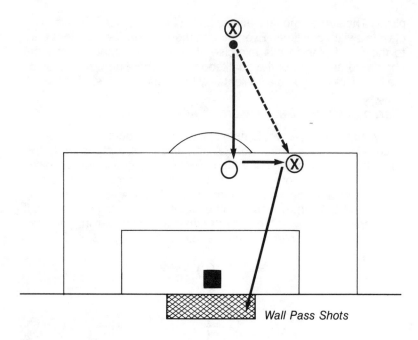

Wall Pass Shots

Three- or More Person Shooting Exercises

Shooting with Many Servers

   With more players, we can have more servers and really give the shooter a workout. The servers, each with a ball, should be spread in a semicircle around the goal area. The shooter stands in the middle. Then one by one, as fast as they can, the servers pass their ball to the shooter. The shooter must either one-touch the ball into the goal with his foot or his head or settle it, turn, and shoot.

Two Versus One or Three Versus Two

   An excellent way to work on offensive and defensive positioning as well as shooting is to set up a two on one or a three on two in front of the goal. This is not the same as the Keep-Away games, but some of the same skills are being tested. Each pair or trio coming down the field should finish their play with a shot on goal, unless, of course, the defense manages to gain control of the ball.

Small-Sided Games

   Some of the small-sided games, three against three or five against five, for example, can emphasize shooting if we place the two goals

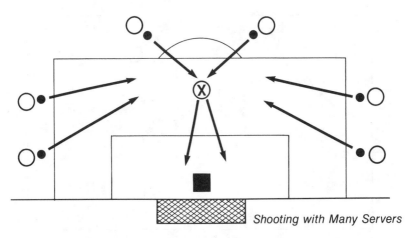

Shooting with Many Servers

especially close together. This way, there is less room for people to pass, and the goal is always within reach for a shot. An affliction often found in less experienced soccer teams is a tendency to "play around" in front of the goal. They pass back and forth, trying to find the perfect shot, and in the meantime, they give the opposing team a

FIG. 7-3 *Two versus one on goal.*

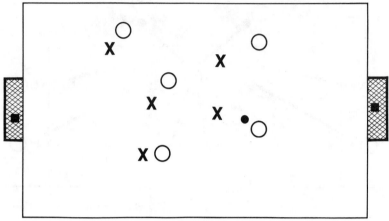

40 YARDS

chance to steal the ball. So, while we like to see players passing on most areas of the field, when they are down in front of the goal, they should find a way to finish. When the goals are brought in tight, the first option is to get off shots and finish. The size of the field is determined by the number of players; for example, twenty yards between the goals for three against three and forty yards for five against five.

A desire to score is essential in the offensive part of the field. Good finishers are the players who *always think of shooting first,* unlike midfielders who have a different mentality; they are more inclined to pass because that is the nature of their position. However, although all good finishers have shooting foremost in their mind, when it's not an option, they will lay it off and become a preparer themselves.

This desire to score is what really gave me my start in soccer. In my very first real game, I was so nervous I couldn't even focus. The blue players looked like red players, and all I could see was a jumble of feet. But my instincts told me I had to put the ball in the goal and that's exactly what I did. It happened to be the only goal scored in the whole game, so the coach had no choice but to try me out in the next game as well. Even though I was still nervous and still playing poorly, I again scored the only goal. This clinched my position on the team.

Rapid Fire

Another drill, which is as much an exercise for the goalkeeper as for the shooters, is to line the balls up on the eighteen-yard line and rapid-fire them at the goal. This exercise will be described in more detail in the next chapter, but it is important for the coaches to stress to the shooters in this drill the importance of kicking the ball out of the reach of the goalie. Because of the rapid-fire shots, the goalie should be off balance fairly often, and the players should *always* take advantage of this.

As we mentioned in the introduction, simply by tacking on a shot to finish the play, a lot of exercises that primarily are used to emphasize other skills can become effective shooting exercises as well.

VIII. Goalkeeping

The Philosophy of Teaching Goalkeeper Basics

The goalkeeper is clearly a very different player from the rest of the players on the team, if for no other reason than that he may use his hands. As a result, I am devoting an entire chapter to exercises that pertain to developing a goalie's skills. But it is important for every coach to realize that this does not mean he should devise a completely separate practice for his goalie. Often it is better to merely include the goalkeeper in the exercises that have been prepared for the whole team.

To remove a goalkeeper from the game situation to teach him how to fly through the air and fall on the ground is fine, but he must also have the game experience, because being able to defend in a game is the bottom line. It won't do a goalie any good to be graceful at leaping through the air if he doesn't know where he should be as the ball is coming down the field. As in everything, matchlike experience is the best teacher.

In addition, keepers who also play on the field have a significant advantage over those whose sole position is in the goal. If the keeper plays on the field, he will have a better concept of the best organization for his defense. He will have an idea when things are going wrong in front of him before the ball gets anywhere near him, and, we hope he will make the adjustments accordingly. If his defensemen are playing as they should, then he knows exactly what the offensive options are for the other team. He knows which shots will come and which ones will be totally useless.

If this sounds as if most of the goalkeeping problems could be resolved by good positioning of the defense, it is because this is absolutely true. If everything in front of the goalkeeper goes right, then his is merely a situation of catching the few shots of no consequence. If a good defense lets a shot get off at all, it will be harmless. But, of course, that's rarely the case. The defense occasionally may not play as well as the opposing team, which gives the attackers many more options. The goalkeeper will have to fly all over the goal to catch up with the mistakes that his defensemen have made.

FIG. 8-1 *Learning to fall. The keeper starts on his knees.*

This is why it is so very important to play the goalkeepers on the field whenever possible and in the goal during small-sided games or appropriate exercises. However, there are also some reasons to isolate the goalies from the rest of the team.

They need to be constantly practicing their skills of jumping and diving. For a keeper to reach the entire goal, he must develop the physical strength to jump, and he must develop the mental toughness to dive and not worry about hurting himself.

A goalkeeper must also learn how to dive and how to keep his hands totally free with the ball. Any goalkeeper who needs his arms or hands for landing is going to be in trouble. He can't dive out to catch a ball if his hands are occupied with breaking his fall. By that time, the ball will be in the net.

Learning to Fall

If a coach wants to teach his goalie to fall, he should start the goalie on his knees. This is best because young goalkeepers need to learn to fall on their sides and use their arms to stop the ball without worrying about hurting themselves. Once they are no longer afraid, then they should stand up. Now the coach should have them fall on

FIG. 8-2A&B *The keeper then must learn to fall from a standing up position.*

their sides, without the ball. They need to get the feel for this, because now that they're higher from the ground they won't be so willing not to use their hands.

Once that is mastered, the next thing to work on is actually diving down; if a keeper merely falls down, he will be too late. Now the coach should bring in the ball and really get the keeper working. The coach should not limit his shots to ground shots, but should also work on chipping the balls. This will seem like a piece of cake for the goalie, but now he has to learn a new skill—when to catch the ball or punch it over the crossbar.

Learning to Use the Hands

Many keepers allow the ball to hit their chests, and then they try to catch it. That is a no-no, and it shows they have not played at a high level before. Hands and arms should be doing the catching; the chest can merely block a shot.

The goalie must always have his hands and thumbs behind the ball so that he can catch it and bring it in. There's a little give that way. It takes some of the velocity off the ball.

FIG. 8-3A *The wrong way to catch a ball.*

FIG. 8-3B *The correct way to catch a ball.*

Sometimes a ball cannot be caught, and if the goalie can't catch the ball and he doesn't do something to get rid of it, it will rebound. Any kind of rebound becomes tremendously dangerous. The best that can be done with these balls is to force them wide or over the top or to punch them out of the area. Another option a goalkeeper has, if there are no attackers nearby, is to slap the ball in front of him. A controlled slap will take the velocity off a ball and place it where the goalie can then pick it up and get on with the play. A keeper cannot do this, obviously, if there is an opponent standing right there to get a foot in. It takes experience to learn which one of these options is best in a given situation.

Rapid Fire

This exact exercise was described in Chapter VII on shooting, but this time the focus is on the goalkeeper. Each player lines up across the eighteen-yard line with a ball. As fast as possible, one after the other shoots on goal.

To begin with, it is helpful to warm up the goalkeeper by making him a target at which the players are supposed to shoot. The keeper makes contact with every ball in a somewhat comfortable manner without having to fly all over the place, because the aim is to warm

FIG. 8-4 *Knocking the ball over the crossbar.*

FIG. 8-5 *Punching the ball out of the way.*

FIG. 8-6 *Slapping the ball down in front.*

FIGURE 8-7A
*Rapid-fire exercises
for the goalkeeper.*

him up. While he gets warmed up, the players get experience target shooting. The players should always begin kicking at about 50 percent of their power and just concentrate on hitting the keeper. When they are warmed up as well, they increase their power up to 100 percent still keeping in mind that they must hit the keeper.

When the goalie is warmed up, the shooters try to maintain this level, yet hit the corners. The coach, however, should be sure to emphasize the importance of scoring over power. There is no use in a powerful shot that goes over the top. The emphasis must always be on scoring.

Now it is the goalkeeper's turn to work. In addition to catching the shooters' hardest shots, the goalkeeper should be forced to work on his different skills. The coach may have him knock all balls over the top or off to the side. He may suggest that the goalie must try to catch them all. He may ask the goalie to punch the balls out of the goal area as best as he can. He may ask the goalie to slap the ball down in front of him. Many of these options will be too difficult for the youngest players (especially if the shooters aren't able to lift the ball in the air); nonetheless, it is good to have them develop a feel for what options they have.

FIG. 8-7B Rapid-fire exercises for the goalkeeper.

FIGURE 8-7C Rapid-fire exercises for the goalkeeper.

Situations

It is good to set up situations for the goalie. Players can serve crosses in from the touchline and force him to defend against them.

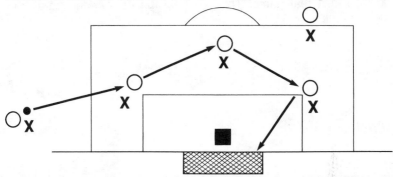

(Legend for Diagrams is in Appendix.)

Corner kicks, penalty kicks, direct kicks, and indirect kicks must all be practiced, and the goalie must know how to defend against all of them. For a direct kick, the additional player in the "wall" will prevent a bending shot from finding the net.

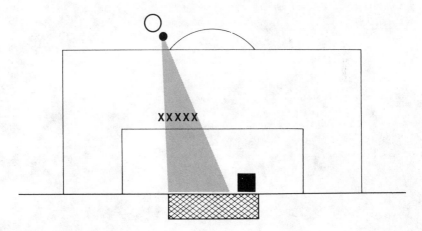

Game Situations

Most important of all, the goalie should practice game situations. First, the coach should begin the exercise with a one-on-one situation, where the goalie must defend against an approaching player without the help of defense. Then the coach adds another offensive player and gives the goalie a defenseman. The coach should continue to add one defensive player and one offensive player and allow the goalie to get used to the different situations he will have to face in a real game. This will help the goalkeeper more than anything else.

IX. Small-Sided Games

Small-sided games encompass many different types of play and don't necessarily mean a miniature scrimmage with equal teams and two goals, although this is a perfectly good description of one type of small-sided game. The games may only have one goal or they may have four goals or they may have no goals at all. They may be played as three versus three up to seven versus seven. The main advantage that each of these exercises has is that they teach tactics. They are often as close to a real match or scrimmage as an exercise is going to get. Every practice should include one or more of these small-sided games, and which game to use will depend on the skill that the coach wishes to emphasize.

In a small-sided exercise, basic concepts—supporting a team-mate defensively, moving to an open space, using a wall pass—often become magnified. It becomes quite obvious, then, who is not performing as expected and who is playing honestly and who can keep up with the flow of the game. It is almost impossible to discover this in a basic skill exercise because there just aren't matchlike conditions.

A small-sided game sets up matchlike conditions, yet it provides the opportunity to stop the play, reset, and, we hope, do it over again correctly. Even more important, it allows the youngsters to learn these tactical skills by performing them.

Five Offense Versus Five Defense

One of the most helpful ways to use a small-sided game situation is to set up five offensive players and five defensive players plus a goalkeeper in front of one goal. In this case, one group of players always plays defense and the other always plays offense. When a play is over (the defense has gained control of the ball), the ball goes back to the coach in the center circle. The players move back to their original positions and the coach feeds the ball to the offense for a new attack. This is helpful if the coach has a specific idea in mind and wants to demonstrate it. It is slightly different from just letting the youngsters play in a matchlike situation. Re-starts like corners, free kicks, and throw-ins in both attack and defense can be worked on as well.

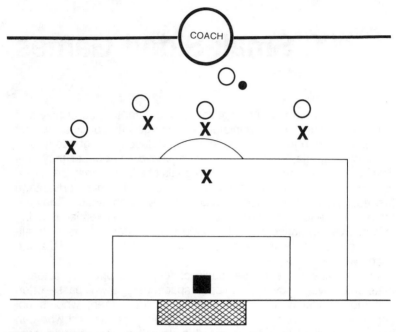

(Legend for Diagrams is in Appendix.)

Keep Away

Keep Away is a game almost every child has played. Surprisingly, it's also one of the best soccer exercises. It can be three against one, two against one, three against two, four against two, five against two, and so on. For the two against one and three against two it should be played with unlimited touches. The overload is not high enough for a one-touch game. The two most useful setups for skill development are the three against one and the five against two.

The three against one should be set up in a limited area marked by four cones. The coach should stress the fact that a player must always have options when he has the ball and it is up to his teammates to give him those options. The players who are on the outside need to keep the game alive by finding shortcuts into the open spaces. They should run in such a way that they never end up behind the defender. The player who is receiving the ball and who will then become the passer can help his two teammates by pointing in the direction that they should run.

Theoretically, it should be very difficult for the defensive player to get the ball. However, for the defensive player to win, he should try to eliminate one passing option by his approach.

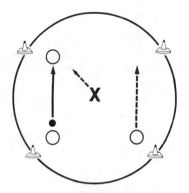 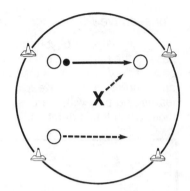

The five versus two is probably the most common type of this Keep Away in soccer, where there are five players on the outside trying to pass to each other and two players in the middle trying to take the ball away. We start off with three- or two-touch and then go to one-touch, depending on how experienced the players are. Working with the advanced players, I like to put them in a ten- or eleven-yard square. At first the players can't believe they will be able to do it, but once they put their mind to it and once they get used to it, they find that it can be done.

It takes tremendous mental sharpness to keep up, because the ball moves so fast and players must constantly readjust within the confines of the tight area. Two players should never be in the same spot, so the players must watch everybody else in addition to the ball.

Not only that, but the players must have the touch to deliver the ball in such a way that the next person doesn't get killed. Or if he has to hit it hard in order to get it through, then the next player must have the ability to take the pace out of it with a soft touch. To speed the ball up, often, is not hard to do, but to slow it down is often a major problem. The beauty of this is that this is exactly what you have to do in the game.

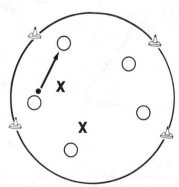

Consecutive Passes for Points

A skill that a lot of youngsters lack is the ability to look for a good pass (if they have the ball) or move into a good position to receive a pass (if they are without the ball). An exercise that helps this is really an elaborate form of Keep Away. The players are divided into two teams and play within a designated area—the smaller the area, the more difficult this game is. There are no goals. A team may only be

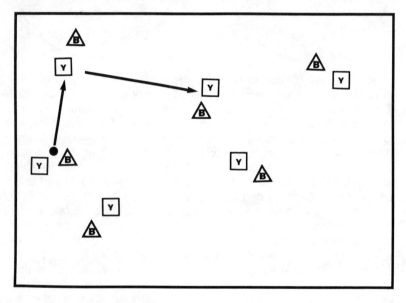

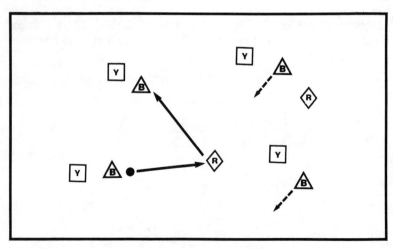

awarded points if it has three (or four or five, depending on level of skill) consecutive passes (passes in which the other team does not touch the ball). Because there are no goals and no specific direction in which the players are supposed to run, they learn to look for open men, to pass backward as well as forward, and to move into an open space in order to receive the ball. In order to make this game even more difficult, a coach can declare that the passes must be two-touch or even one-touch. In that case, the coach should add one or two additional players who constantly play on the side that has the ball. For instance, the yellow team plays against the blue team, but the two red-shirted players play with both, depending on which team has the ball.

Four Goals

Believe it or not, one of the best exercises for defense and attack involves four goals. This is best done with a three versus three or four versus four or five versus five. There are only two teams and each

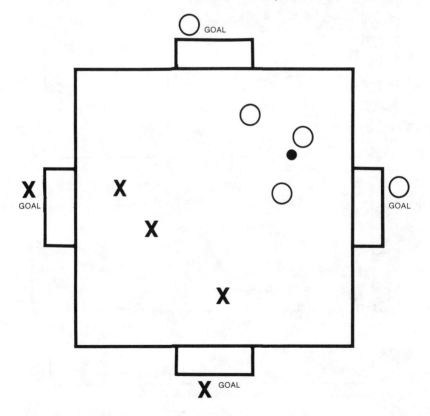

team must defend two adjacent goals. The strategy here is for the players to fake the attack toward one goal and then head toward the other one. This exercise really forces the youngsters to be alert, to watch the players moving in all parts of the field, and to play both defense and offense, no matter what their starting position was.

The Number Game

The number game is pretty simple, and it is played between two goals in a fairly small area. If, for example, there are two teams of seven, the coach should give each person on each team a number from one to seven. The coach then calls one of these numbers, and the two players with those numbers play a one-on-one game against each other, with a goalie in each goal. The others stand next to the

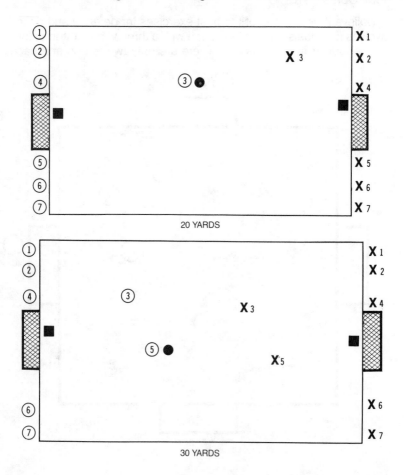

20 YARDS

30 YARDS

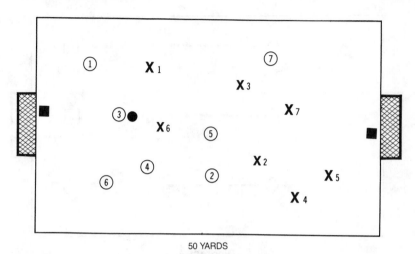

50 YARDS

goal. After all have played a one-on-one, the coach calls out two numbers. Now it becomes a two-against-two game, and it can go all the way up to where it is seven against seven. The only concern with the bigger numbers is that the field should be expanded by moving the portable goals farther apart.

Three Versus Three Versus Three

This is a two-goal game that should be fairly self-explanatory from the name—it involves a three against three against three—but it is a little more complicated to set up. This should be played in a somewhat larger area than the last exercise. The three teams spread across the field in lines, parallel to one another. There should be one team in front of each goal (in Diagram A, the triangles and the squares) and the third team (the diamonds) should be in the middle of the field between them. The team in the middle (diamond) starts with the ball. They are the offense first and will head toward one goal to try to score. The team they head toward (square) is, for now, the defensive team (Diagram A). When the defensive team gets the ball (or if the ball goes out of bounds or into the goal), that team (square) becomes the offensive team and heads down the field toward the third team in front of the other goal (Diagram B). This third team (triangle) now plays defense to the second (square) team's offense. The three players who started in the middle (diamond) and were just playing offense rest in front of the first goal as they wait for the ball to come back, at which time they will play defense (Diagram C). The cycle just keeps going, with the teams switching from offense to defense all the time. This game can also be done as four against four, although it is less complicated with three on each team.

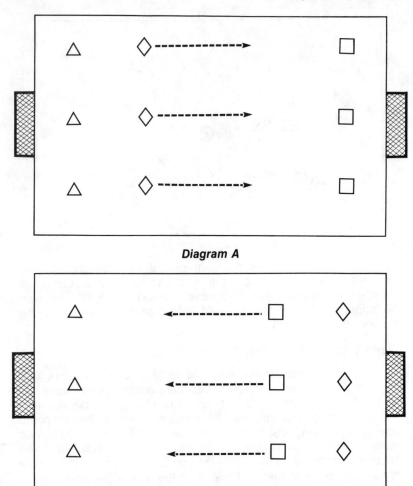

Diagram A

Diagram B

Players Are the Goals

For this exercise, the youngsters should be divided into groups of four. Two of the players stand about twenty yards apart from each other and spread their legs. They are the goals. The other two play a one-on-one game against each other. To score, they must put the ball through the legs of one of the goals. This is a good exercise to do for time. The first pair should play for two minutes, then they get two

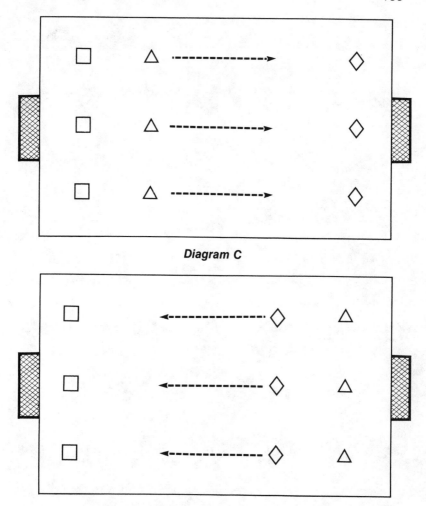

Diagram C

minutes to rest as they become the goals and the people who were the goals become the one-on-one players.

Small-sided games are the main reason why training sessions are successful. It is mandatory, therefore, that the coach use some of these games in his practice.

X. Wrap-Up

To write a book on soccer is like playing the game itself. We always have the feeling that it was not perfect and we hope to do it a little better the next time. What I have tried to do in this book is to give the new coach a variety of exercises that can be as useful for five-year-olds as for professional soccer players.

Most of these exercises can be taken from a very basic level to a matchlike competition. The importance of this progression cannot be emphasized enough. This mirrors the development of a player.

Again and again I have stressed how important the basics are. Only when the basics are working well for him should a player try more daring moves with higher risks. Players with limited skills or a limited ability to "read" the game often complicate matters, both for their teammates and for themselves, by attempting difficult maneuvers when a simple one would suffice. Why should a player flip the ball over his head if a simple pass will accomplish the same thing?

Mastering the basics and learning how to "read" the game is what we as coaches hope to accomplish by placing the youngster in a more gamelike situation during practices. If a youngster is merely doing a drill, he will not be forced to improvise. For the offensive players especially, improvisation and daring are essential. Good players know when to take risks and when to play it safe, but they don't learn this until they play a game. A constant challenge exists between the game in its basic nature and the players who attempt to play it. Or, to put it a little differently, the demands of the game in comparison to the players' strengths and limitations take center stage in the athletic drama.

All the top players that soccer has ever known have one thing in common. They can keep matters simple and play with a high level of control. A statement one of my colleagues likes to use makes a lot of sense: When things are not going well, look at the basics for repair and improvement. The great masters of the game are often sticklers for detail. The degree of excellence in the basics counts for more than the ability to be spectacular.

Good players also focus on their strengths and practice them as often as possible. On a good team, a player's weaknesses will be masked by the blending of different players with different skills. This is the essence of teamwork, and this is the essence of soccer.

Appendix

Legend

●   Ball

○   Offense or Server

X   Defense

■   Goalie

━━━━   Movement of ball

▪▬▬▬▪   Movement of player

●▬●   Dribbling

🔺   Cone

Ⓧ   Shooter

□   Player

△   Player

◇   Player

Soccer's Organizational Setup

Soccer is the world's most popular team sport. It is played, and enjoys huge fan support, in all countries of the globe.

Soccer is governed, world-wide, by the FEDERATION INTERNA-TIONALE de FOOTBALL ASSOCIATION (referred to as the F.I.F.A.), which has its permanent world-headquarters in Switzerland. The laws governing all team-soccer activities are established by this international organization and adhered to world-wide.

F.I.F.A. has various regional governing organizations under its control. The one we are assigned to is called CONCACAF and covers Central and North America; the others are found in Europe, Asia, Africa, and South America.

The United States, under these governing bodies, is controlled by the UNITED STATE SOCCER FEDERATION (USSF), which maintains its National Headquarters in Colorado Springs, Colorado, its Youth Administrative National Headquarters in Memphis, Tennessee, and its Senior Amateur Headquarters in Bergen County, New Jersey. Our country is split into four regions, North, South, East and West, for both junior and senior administrative purposes. Within each Region you have the respective Senior and Junior State Associations; below the State Associations, and as their members, you have the various local leagues, made up of clubs and teams. In addition, and operating separately within the USSF, you have the Intercollegiate Soccer Association, the National Coaches Association and the National Referees Association.

Whenever we wish to qualify for world soccer championships—irrespective of age group selected and unless we are the host nation—our national team is required to beat, within our Regional International Area, the other members of CONCACAF, which are Canada, Mexico, Costa Rica, Bermuda, Puerto Rico, Trinidad and Tobago, Guatemala, Honduras, Nicaragua, Panama, Haiti, Jamaica, Bahamas, Dominican Republic, Cuba and Guadeloupe.

Harry J. Saunders

Soccer Seasons

The playing season for the educational teams of the United States (colleges and schools) is much too short, hindering the proper development of top players and their respective teams. Progress can only be attained through constant experience, namely competition.

Other nations around the world offer players of all age categories an approximate nine-month season, with June, July and August being considered the off-season. Most teams play one game a week, sometimes two if a cup-match is added.

At least two separate training sessions should be held each week, both during the season and about four weeks prior to the commencement of a seasonal championship tournament.

Harry J. Saunders

MANFRED SCHELLSCHEIDT

Manfred "Manny" Schellscheidt, head soccer coach of Seton Hall University, is in his fourth decade of playing and coaching soccer at the highest amateur and professional levels. He helped guide the Philadelphia Atoms to the North American League title and the Rhode Island Oceaneers and the New Jersey Americans to American League titles, and was head coach of the North American Soccer League's Hartford Bicentennials. He was head coach of the United States 1984 Olympic Team and two editions (1975 and 1983) of the United States Pan American Team. His youth league coaching experience includes stints as assistant coach of the 1985 National Youth Team Under 16, which participated in World Cup play in China; head coach of the Union (NJ) Lancers, a 19-and-under club team which captured the 1987 and 1988 McGwire Cup as national champions; and head coach of various New Jersey State Select Teams since 1980. In addition to heading Seton Hall's perennial collegiate Top-10 soccer program, Manny has coached or played on four amateur national championship teams since 1970. He holds the highest soccer coaching certificate in both the United States and West Germany, is a member of the National Coaching Staff of the U.S. Soccer Federation and a 1967 graduate of the University of Sports in Cologne, West Germany.

DEBORAH WICKENDEN

Deborah Wickenden is a free-lance writer and editor living in Boston, Massachusetts. She played four years of varsity soccer for Williams College and two years in the New York State Women's Soccer League. She has coached 10 and 11 year old boys and girls, and currently coaches 8 and 9 year old girls in the Boston Area Youth Soccer league.

Credits
Book Production/Design: Mountain Lion, Inc.
Cover Design: Michael Bruner
Copyediting: Jean Atcheson
Photographs: Michael Plunkett
Typesetting: Elizabeth Typesetting Company
Mechanical: Production Graphics
Cover Photograph © Mountain Lion/John Monteleone